THE GLENCOE LITERATURE LIBRARY

Cyrano de Bergerac

and Related Readings

Glencoe
McGraw-Hill

New York, New York   Columbus, Ohio   Woodland Hills, California   Peoria, Illinois

Acknowledgments

Grateful acknowledgment is given authors, publishers, photographers, museums, and agents for permission to reprint the following copyrighted material. Every effort has been made to determine copyright owners. In case of any omissions, the Publisher will be pleased to make suitable acknowledgments in future editions.

CYRANO DE BERGERAC by Edmond Rostand, translated and adapted for the stage by Anthony Burgess. The amateur and stock performance rights to this work are controlled exclusively by Applause Theatre Books, Inc., without whose permission in writing no performance of it may be given. Royalty arrangements and licenses must be secured well in advance of presentation. Royalty must be paid every time a play is performed whether or not it is presented for profit and whether or not admission is charged. A play is performed anytime it is read or acted before an audience. All inquiries concerning amateur, stock, and first class rights should be addressed to Applause Books, Licensing Division, 211 West 71st Street, New York, NY, 10023, fax # (212) 721-2856.

No alterations, deletions or substitutions may be made in the work without the prior written consent of the publisher. No part of this work may be reproduced or transmitted in any form or by any means, electronic or mechanical, including photocopy, recording, videotape, film, or any information storage and retrieval system, without permission in writing from the publisher. On all programs, printing and advertising for the play this notice must appear: "Produced by special arrangement with Applause Theatre Books."

Due authorship credit must be given on all programs, printing and advertising for the play.

Reprinted by arrangement with Applause Theatre Books.

Text excerpt, "Chapter 4, The Masterpieces" from EDMOND ROSTAND by Alba della Fazia Amoia, copyright © 1978, G. K. Hall & Co. (Twayne Publishers), pp. 60–70, 72–75. Reprinted by permission of the Gale Group.

Text excerpts, "Cyrano de Bergerac" and " 'Cyrano' in English" from AROUND THEATRES by Max Beerbohm, copyright © 1969 by Taplinger Publishing Co., Inc., pp. 4–7, 73–75.

"Beauty: When the Other Dancer Is the Self" by Alice Walker, from *Ms. Magazine*, May 1983. Copyright © Alice Walker. Reprinted by permission of the Wendy Weil Agency.

"Strangers in Love" from ONLINE SEDUCTIONS: Falling in Love with Strangers on the Internet by Esther Gwinnell, M.D., copyright © 1998, Kodansha International Co., pp. 1–15, 19. Reprinted by permission.

Cover Art: Pushkin Museum of Fine Arts, Moscow/Superstock

Glencoe/McGraw-Hill

*A Division of The **McGraw·Hill** Companies*

Send all inquiries to:
Glencoe/McGraw-Hill
8787 Orion Place
Columbus, OH 43240

ISBN 0-02-817989-7
Printed in the United States of America
2 3 4 5 6 7 8 9 026 04 03 02 01 00

Contents

Cyrano de Bergerac

Related Readings   147

Continued

Contents *Continued*

Cyrano de Bergerac

Edmond Rostand

translated and adapted for the modern stage by
Anthony Burgess

The Characters

Named

CYRANO DE BERGERAC

CHRISTIAN DE NEUVILLETTE

COMTE DE GUICHE

RAGUENEAU

LE BRET

CARBON DE CASTEL-JALOUX

VICOMTE DE VALVERT

MONTFLEURY

BELLEROSE

JODELET

CUIGY

LIGNIÈRE

BRISSAILLE

THÉOPHRASTE RENAUDOT

BERTRANDOU THE FLUTEPLAYER

ROXANE

LISE

MOTHER MARGUÉRITE DE JÉSUS

SISTER MARTHE

SISTER CLAIRE

Unnamed

DOORKEEPER

A CAVALRYMAN

A MUSKETEER

ANOTHER MUSKETEER

(believed to be d'Artagnan)

A GUARD

A FAT MAN

A CITIZEN

HIS SON

A DRUNKARD

A PICKPOCKET

HIS APPRENTICES

TWO FLUNKEYS

TWO BOYS

(pages at the theatre, customers at
Ragueneau's shop, eventually
musicians)

OTHER PAGES

TWO MARQUISES

A CAPUCHIN

A SENTRY

THE POETS

A POET

PASTRYCOOKS

CADETS

A SPANISH OFFICER

ROXANE'S DUENNA

(eventually Sister Marthe)

FLOWERGIRL

FOODSELLER

ACTRESSES

THE CROWD,
MARQUISES, THIEVES,
ACTORS, MUSICIANS,
PRÉCIEUSES, NUNS, ETC.

Act 1

A theatre

[*We are in Paris in 1640, the era of Dumas's* Three Musketeers. *The theatre is not a theatre as we know theatres. It is rather like a large indoor tennis court roughly converted into a place where plays may be performed before small audiences, or chamber concerts given for even fewer. There is a platform which serves as a stage, and a number of benches accommodate the less patrician spectators. The gentry and aristocracy will be seated in a low gallery with chairs, while a higher one, chairless, from which the view is not good, is intended for their servants. It is evening. The lights have not yet been lit, and a huge candelabrum has still to be raised by its heavy rope to the ceiling. The shadows invite lovers and lechers. Such illumination as there is is provided by odd candles and lanterns set about the floor and on chairs. A* PICKPOCKET *instructs his pupils in the art they must practise this evening. A* DOORKEEPER *takes tickets or, from the ticketless, money. A* CAVALRYMAN *pushes his way in past him.*]

DOORKEEPER.   Hey—where's your fifteen sous?

CAVALRYMAN.   I get in free.

DOORKEEPER.   And why?

CAVALRYMAN.   His Majesty's Household Cavalry.

[*Another man in uniform enters boldly. He is a* MUSKETEER.]

DOORKEEPER.   You—

MUSKETEER.   I don't pay either.

DOORKEEPER.   Now look here—

MUSKETEER.   *You* look, friend. See—I'm a musketeer.

CAVALRYMAN.   [*to the* MUSKETEER.]
5   Ten minutes before curtain-up. The floor
        Is ours.

MUSKETEER.   So—what are we waiting for?

[*They draw their épées and start to fence. A* FLUNKEY *comes out of the shadows to watch them. Another* FLUNKEY *appears and addresses the first.*]

SECOND FLUNKEY.   Psst—see what I've got—

[*It is not easy to see what he has in the dimness.*]

FIRST FLUNKEY.   Champagne?

SECOND FLUNKEY.   Cards. Dice.
    What'll it be?

FIRST FLUNKEY.   [*taking the cards.*]
                I'll deal.

SECOND FLUNKEY.   I nicked a slice
    Of candle. See.

[*He lights it from a candle already lighted and sticks it on a bench.*]

                    See.

[*Now they can see well enough to play. A town* GUARD *appears from the shadows and makes for a* FLOWERGIRL *who has just come in with her basket of spring blooms.*]

GUARD.   Come on—here's a nice
10   Little bit of dark, dear. Give us a kiss.

CAVALRYMAN.   [*lunging.*]   *Touché!*

GUARD.   [*embracing her.*]
    Come on.

FLOWERGIRL.   They can see.

FIRST FLUNKEY.   One club.

GUARD.   No danger.

[*A* FAT MAN, *seated, takes out a cold fowl and a loaf.*]

FAT MAN.   May
    As well get a snack in.

[*A* CITIZEN, *decently but drably dressed, enters with his* SON, *a lad of about seventeen, drably but decently dressed. The* CITIZEN *peers in the dim light.*]

CITIZEN.   Come on, son—this way.

DRUNKARD.   [*to the eater.*]
    What's this place called, then?

FAT MAN.   Theatre Beaujolais.

[*The* DRUNKARD *produces a bottle.*]

DRUNKARD.   A good idea.

SECOND FLUNKEY.   Three aces.

CITIZEN.   [*indignantly.*]   You'd think that this
15   Was a brothel—

GUARD.   Come on, give us a kiss.

CITIZEN.   God in heaven—playing cards where they play Corneille.

HIS SON.   Racine as well.

[*The* GUARD *gets his kiss, a long one, and the* CITIZEN *sees it.*]

CITIZEN.   Son, look the other way.

SON.   Racine's a bit of a bore, though, to be truthful.

[*Some* PAGES *enter, singing a rude song.* THE DOORKEEPER *looks on them with disapproval.*]

DOORKEEPER.   All right, you pages, cut that out.

FIRST PAGE.   Just youthful
20   Exuberance, monsieur.

SECOND PAGE.   String?

FIRST PAGE.   [*showing a length of it and also. . . .*]
                And a hook.

DOORKEEPER.   [*muttering.*]   Young pigs.

SECOND PAGE.   Let's get up there and start to fish for wigs.

[*They boisterously make their way to the upper gallery. The* PICKPOCKET *addresses his* APPRENTICES *weightily.*]

PICKPOCKET.   Now, you young villains, novices in crime,
    You're performing in public for the very first time—

SECOND PAGE.   Peashooters at the ready—

THIRD PAGE.   Launch your peas.

[*The first and second* PAGES *hit pates with their peashooters. The* DOORKEEPER *shakes a furious fist at them.*]

25   CITIZEN'S SON.   I've forgotten what they're doing tonight.

CITIZEN.   Clorise.

PICKPOCKET.   Don't cut the lace too close. The important factor's
    Lightness of touch.

CITIZEN.   With some really exquisite actors—

PICKPOCKET.   Now, as for nicking watches—

CITIZEN.   Yes, you'll see
Montfleury—

PICKPOCKET.   Tonight, watch me—

CITIZEN.   Bellerose, L'Épy—

30   VOICE.   Lights! Lights!

CITIZEN.   Le Beaupré, Jodelet—

FIRST PAGE.   There she is!

[*He means a very pretty girl who has appeared from the shadows with a trolley on which food and drink are set.*]

FOODSELLER.   Cider, raspberry cordial, oranges!

FIRST MARQUIS.   [*off.*]
Make way, there!

[*He enters with another MARQUIS. After these enter CUIGY and BRISSAILLE, mere gentlemen, and, a little after, LIGNIÈRE, a poet who has the face of a distinguished drunkard. He accompanies CHRISTIAN DE NEUVILLETTE, a young baron from the north, very handsome, soldierly, his civilian dress somewhat out of the fashion.*]

FIRST FLUNKEY.   What's this?—marquises?—in the pit?

SECOND MARQUIS.   Make room, will you? Animals!

SECOND FLUNKEY.   Oh, just for a bit.
Then they get sort of elevated.

FIRST MARQUIS.   Scum.
35   It's positively obscene, really, to come
In early like this with the shopkeepers. Why,
There aren't even any decent feet to tread on. Ah, Brissaille,
Cuigy—

[*Affectionate greetings.*]

CUIGY.   My dear. We're here with the devout,
Before even the candles are lit.

FIRST MARQUIS.   Pooh!

SECOND MARQUIS.   Come, don't pout.
40   The lights are coming on now.

[*So they are. The candelabrum is illuminated with care and raised during what follows. LIGNIÈRE is now clearly visible.*]

CUIGY.   Ah, Lignière!

LIGNIÈRE.　　[*to* CHRISTIAN.]
　　An introduction?

[CHRISTIAN *shrugs, then nods.*]

BRISSAILLE.　　[*to* LIGNIÈRE.]
　　　　　　　　Not under the table yet?

[LIGNIÈRE *ignores the remark and formally introduces* CHRISTIAN.]

LIGNIÈRE.　　May I present the Baron de Neuvillette?

[*The crowd expresses its delight by going 'Aaaah!' as the lights grow brighter and brighter. The* MARQUISES *and* CUIGY *appraise* CHRISTIAN.]

CUIGY.　　A charming head of hair on the boy, yes?

FIRST MARQUIS.　　[*doubtfully.*]　　　　　　　　Well—

LIGNIÈRE.　　　　　　　　　　　　　　　　　Messieurs
　　De Cuigy, de Brissaille—

CHRISTIAN.　　　　　　　*Enchanté.*

FIRST MARQUIS.　　　　　　　Pretty
45　　Enough, but rather provincial.

SECOND MARQUIS.　　　　Hm, a pity.

[LIGNIÈRE *hears the remark about* CHRISTIAN'S *provinciality.*]

LIGNIÈRE.　　The baron comes from Touraine.

CUIGY.　　　　　　　　　　　　Really?

CHRISTIAN.　　　　　　　　　　　　Well, yes

CUIGY.　　A stranger to Paris?

CHRISTIAN.　　　　　　　I've been here rather less
　　Than three weeks.

[*These aristocrats fluster him, and he has something else on his mind.*]
　　　　　　　　I'm joining the Guards.

[*The ladies of wit and fashion have arrived and are taking their places in the lower gallery.*]

FIRST MARQUIS.　　　　　　　　　　There she is—
　　Madame Aubry.

FOODSELLER.　　Lemonade, oranges.

STRINGS.　　[*tuning up.*]
50　　La. La. Laaaaaa—

CUIGY.　　[*to Christian.*]
　　　　　　Quite a crowd here, eh?

CHRISTIAN. Indeed.

FIRST MARQUIS. The *bon ton.*

SECOND MARQUIS. Madame de Guéméné—

CUIGY. DeBois-Dauphin—

FIRST MARQUIS. Whom once we were crazy for—

BRISSAILLE. De Chauvigny—

SECOND MARQUIS. Who treats our hearts like the floor.

LIGNIÈRE. Corneille has come from Rouen.

CITIZEN. The Academy?
55 There they are, most of them. Can you see?
Boudu, Boissat, Cureau, Forchères, Colomby,
Bourzeys, Bourdon, Arbaud—what an honour to sit
Near names that can never die. Just think of it.

[*We cannot see these personages, since they are all somewhere in our auditorium. We are not missing much, however. But we do see the very special ladies of wit and fashion now enter.*]

FIRST MARQUIS. Ah, here they come—our *précieuses*—

CHRISTIAN. [*to LIGNIÈRE.*] What are
those?

60 **LIGNIÈRE.** Beautiful bluestockings.

CHRISTIAN. [*mystified.*] What?

FIRST MARQUIS. Ah—there she goes.
Barthénoide, and there's Félixérie—
Urimédonte, Cassadance—

LIGNIÈRE. To me
They sound like high-class diseases.

SECOND MARQUIS. [*to FIRST MARQUIS.*] Exquisite
Pseudonyms. You know them all?

FIRST MARQUIS. I admit
65 To trying to know them all.

LIGNIÈRE. [*somewhat irritably, to CHRISTIAN.*]
Look, I came here
To help you if I could. But it's pretty clear
That the lady isn't coming. I'll be on my way—
I've some serious drinking to do tonight.

CHRISTIAN. [*urgently.*]   No, stay
　　　Just a while longer. *Please.* To nurse a flame
70　　Like mine for a . . .

[*He has difficulty, as always, in finding the right word.*]

　　　LIGNIÈRE.   Woman without a name?

[*The ORCHESTRA LEADER has come in, to no applause. He chins his fiddle, raises his bow.*]

　　　ORCHESTRA LEADER.   Gentlemen of the orchestra—

[*He gives the downbeat, and they play soft preludial music.*]

　　　FOODSELLER.   Lemonade.
　　　Macaroons.

　　　CHRISTIAN.   You'll know her. I'm afraid,
　　　Afraid she'll be coquettish, exquisite—
　　　Afraid to speak and show my . . .

　　　LIGNIÈRE.   Lack of wit.

75　CHRISTIAN.   This smart new language they all speak and write
　　　Eludes me. All I know is . . .

　　　LIGNIÈRE. [*promptly.*]   How to fight.
　　　A soldier conqueredby two enemies—
　　　Shyness and love.

　　　CHRISTIAN.   I *must* know who she is.
　　　Wait till she comes—she's bound to come—

　　　LIGNIÈRE.   Oh, no.
80　　Thirst waits for no man. Sorry, I must go—
　　　I've the whole of Paris to swim through.

[*The FOODSELLER brightly accosts him.*]

　　　FOODSELLER.   Orangeade?

　　　LIGNIÈRE. [*shuddering.*] Oh God.

　　　FOODSELLER.   Milk?

　　　LIGNIÈRE.   My sweet young dairymaid,
　　　I was weaned a long long time back.

　　　FOODSELLER.   Muscadel?

　　　LIGNIÈRE.   Hm. Sweetish, sweetish. Very well,
85　　Christian, I'll stay awhile.

[*He sits on the edge of a bench and the* FOODSELLER *pours him a large glass. Meanwhile* RAGUENEAU *has entered—portly, dressed in a Sunday suit, well pleased with himself, acknowledging the recognition of the crowd.*]

LIGNIÈRE.   Ah, Ragueneau.
[*To* CHRISTIAN.]
This is the man who lets you eat and owe,
If you're a poet.

RAGUENEAU.   Monsieur Lignière,
Have you seen Monsieur de Bergerac anywhere?

LIGNIÈRE.   The prince of pastrycooks.

RAGUENEAU.   Oh, really, now—

90   LIGNIÈRE.   Quiet, you patron of the tarts, arts.

RAGUENEAU.   I allow
That poets honour my establishment.

LIGNIÈRE.   On credit.
He's a talented poet himself.

RAGUENEAU.   Well, some have said it.

LIGNIÈRE.   Cracked, aren't you, crazy about the art?

RAGUENEAU.   Well—

LIGNIÈRE.   For an ode he'll pay a rhubarb tart.

95   RAGUENEAU.   Let's say a tartlet.

LIGNIÈRE.   And a sonnet?

RAGUENEAU.   A small Swiss roll.

LIGNIÈRE.   As for a play—

RAGUENEAU.   The drama—ah, my soul
Seethes.

LIGNIÈRE.   Damp your oven, sir. Gâteaux and such
Buy him his theatre tickets. Tell us how much
It cost you to come tonight.

RAGUENEAU.   Four fruit flans,
100   Six cream buns. Where's Cyrano?

LIGNIÈRE.   That man's
Not much of a theatregoer.

[*He is now on his third glass.*]

RAGUENEAU.   Oh, but he's
    Got to be here.

LIGNIÈRE.   *Got* to be?

RAGUENEAU.   Montfluery's
    Performing.

LIGNIÈRE.   True, treading a tragic measure,
    Three hundred pounds of pork *en gelée*. So?

105 **RAGUENEAU.**   Cyrano has warned him—surely you know?—
    To quit the stage on pain of his displeasure
    For a whole month.

BRISSAILLE.   And, to quote Lignière, so?

RAGUENEAU.   Montfleury's performing.

CUIGY.   An empty sort of veto,
    Surely.

RAGUENEAU.   I think not, gentlemen, oh no.
110   That's why I'm here. Where is he?

FIRST MARQUIS.   This Cyrano—
    What is he?

CUIGY.   A sort of metal merchant.

SECOND MARQUIS.   Oh,
    Not aristocratic, then?

CUIGY.   Sufficiently so.
    He's in the Guards. But there's his friend Le Bret.

[*He refers to a good solid captain of the* GUARDS, *who is pacing up and down nervously.*]

    Le Bret, come over. What have you to say
115   About this Cyrano business?

[*LE BRET comes over to the group.*]

LE BRET.   Oh God.

CUIGY.   I see.

LE BRET.   I'm worried.

BRISSAILLE.   You have every right to be.

[*But* RAGUENEAU *has been smiling.*]

RAGUENEAU.   What an extraordinary man he is.

LE BRET.   Exquisite—one of the world's prodigies.

RAGUENEAU. Poet.

CUIGY. Fighter.

BRISSAILLE. Physician.

LE BRET. Musician.

LIGNIÈRE. Ah—
120 His appearance, though—isn't that truly bizarre?

RAGUENEAU. Bizarre, excessive, hyperbolic, droll,
With his triple-waving plume, his visible soul,
Six slashes in his doublet, and his cloak,
Which the flashing scabbard hoists up at the back
125 To make it like the tail of a barnyard cock—
That is Cyrano de Bergerac.
Cocky, insolent, Gascony-proud he goes,
Flaunting that Punchinello strawberry nose
Of his—a nose, gentlemen, that makes one feel
130 Like squealing: 'Oh God, no, it can't be real.
It must be detachable—*is*, I'm prepared to bet.'
But Cyrano's never been known to detach it yet.

LE BRET. He wears it, or it him, and, should anyone laugh,
His sword swoops down and lops him clean in half.

135 RAGUENEAU. The blade is one of the blades of destiny's scissors.

FIRST MARQUIS. But he doesn't seem to be coming.

LE BRET. Oh, yes he is, as
Sure as my name's—

RAGUENEAU. He'll be here in a minute or so.
I'm prepared to bet a *poulet Ragueneau*.

[*To universal admiration* ROXANE *enters with her* DUENNA. CHRISTIAN, *who is paying for* LIGNIÈRE'S *wine, does not see her. But everybody else does.*]

SECOND MARQUIS. Look at her—how unbearably beautiful—

140 FIRST MARQUIS. A strawberry mouth in peach-flesh.

SECOND MARQUIS. So fresh, so cool,
She'd give one cardiac rheumatism.

[CHRISTIAN *sees her, is speechless, clutches* LIGNIÈRE *and points tremulously.*]

LIGNIÈRE. Ah, so
That's the one.

CHRISTIAN.   Yes yes yes, who? Tell me—oh,
    My knees are knocking.

LIGNIÈRE.   Second name—Robin.
    Known as Roxane, though christened Madeleine.

CHRISTIAN.   [*ardently.*]
145   Roxane!

LIGNIÈRE.   Roxana really. You know—
    Alexander's mistress.

[CHRISTIAN, *in a transport of jealousy, prepares to draw his sword.*]

CHRISTIAN.   Alexander!

LIGNIÈRE.   Wait.
    He's dead. He's safe. He used to be called the Great.
    Delicately reared. Bookish.

CHRISTIAN.   Bookish? Oh no.

LIGNIÈRE.   Still single. An orphan. Cousin to the Cyrano
150   We were talking about just now.

[*A nobleman is to be seen paying her every courtly attention.*]

CHRISTIAN.   Who's that with her?

[LIGNIÈRE *takes a deep draught and then launches into alexandrines.*]

LIGNIÈRE.   That's the Comte de Guiche, complete with *cordon bleu,*
    Totally smitten with her but irreparably wed
    To the niece of none other than Cardinal Richelieu.
    If he can't marry Roxane, he proposes to hitch her instead
155   To a certain unpleasant viscount—there he is—Valvert.
    The viscount is—complaisant. So de Guiche will push in there
    If you catch my meaning. She comes of the bourgeoisie,
    And de Guiche could unleash, if he wished, such concentrated hell
    As to make her wish she'd never been born. Ah well,
160   That's de Guiche, the swine. He has it in for me.
    I wrote a little song about him showing
    Up his piggish machiavellianisms. I'll sing it.

CHRISTIAN.   No, I'm going
    To to to—

[*But* LIGNIÈRE *with drunkard's strength holds on to him.*]

LIGNIÈRE.   You're going to listen. Listen.

[*He sings in a cracked voice.*]

The bite of that
165 Aristocrat,
Like any other sewer rat,
Infects the gut
With such a glut
Of venom in the groin or gut
170 That, so they tell,
The victims yell
Not from the pain but from the smell.

[CHRISTIAN *tears himself away.*]

CHRISTIAN.   Let's get it over now, once and for ever—

LIGNIÈRE.   Who?

CHRISTIAN.   This Viscount de Valvert.

LIGNIÈRE.   Idiot. Small stuff like you—
175 He'll eat you in canapés. Stop it. And see—
She's looking at you.

CHRISTIAN.   [*enraptured.*]   Oh heavens, it's true.
At me. At me. God, she's looking at me.

LIGNIÈRE.   So—me and my thirst—we'll be the ones to go.

[He *zigzags off. The chief* PICKPOCKET *takes advantage of* CHRISTIAN'S *ecstasy to sidle towards him. The* APPRENTICE PICKPOCKETS *look at their master's behest. A lesson.*]

LE BRET.   No Cyrano.

RAGUENEAU.   I can't understand it.

LE BRET.   Oh,
180 It's possible he hasn't seen the playbill.

[*The* SPECTATORS *are growing impatient. They yell.*]

SPECTATORS.   Begin! Begin! Begin!

LE BRET.   I hope that's so.

FIRST MARQUIS.   Keeps quite a court, de Guiche.

[DE GUICHE *is indeed the centre of a number of sycophants. He stands chatting with them at the pit level in front of the lower gallery.*]

SECOND MARQUIS.   Another one
Of these Gascons—supple, cold, able.
No doubt about it, marquis, they get on.
185 Shall we pay our respects?

[*The other nods and they trip over to* DE GUICHE *to admire his exquisite clothes.*]

FIRST MARQUIS.   Such lovely ribbons, sir.
    What is this colour called? Kiss-me-my-dear?
    Or startled-fawn?

DE GUICHE.   Sick Spaniard.

SECOND MARQUIS.   Ah, that colour
    Tells no lie. Thanks to your lordship's valour,
    The Spanish force in Flanders, so we hear,
190   Will soon be very sick.

DE GUICHE.   I must take my place
    Up there. Coming?

[*He goes towards the stage where, in the Elizabethan manner, chairs are set for a few of the better sort. He sees* VALVERT *hanging back, eyes on* ROXANE.]

                      Coming? Coming, Valvert?

[VALVERT *shakes himself out of his absorption and follows his patron. Hearing the name,* CHRISTIAN *trembles with rage.*]

CHRISTIAN. Good as dead. Let me hurl it in his face,
    My—

[*He puts his hand in his pocket but finds the* PICKPOCKET's *already there. The neophytes are shocked by their master's ineptitude.*]

PICKPOCKET. [*amiably.*]
        Quite a crush tonight. We're practically
    In one another's pockets.

CHRISTIAN.   So I see.
195   I was looking for a glove.

PICKPOCKET.   And you've found a mitt.

[*His sick and piteous smirk changes. He speaks urgently.*]

    I didn't have no intention—It was just a bit
    Of (ow!) fun—

[CHRISTIAN *holds on to the mitt, hard.*]

            Let me go, sir, and I'll let
    (Ow!) you into a secret—

CHRISTIAN.   Secret? What? *What*?

[*He hangs on to the hand but lets it gradually go during the following.*]

PICKPOCKET.   That Lignière—him who's just left—he's not
200   Got more that an hour to live. He wrote a song
          Attacking one of these gents, who's sending along
          A hundred men to get him. I'm one. That's how
          I know, you see?

CHRISTIAN.   What 'gent'?

PICKPOCKET.   Oh really, now—
          Professional discretion—

CHRISTIAN.   Where will they be?

205   PICKPOCKET.   The porte de Nesle. That's on his way home, see.
          You'd better get a message to him.

CHRISTIAN.   How
          Am I going to find him?

PICKPOCKET.   Start off now.
          Try all the public houses—The Red Cow,
          The Broken Corset, Pineapple—try the lot,
210   Jot down a message. Quick, though. Soon he'll not
          Be able to read.

[*Freed, the* PICKPOCKET *shamefacedly returns to his little troupe.* CHRISTIAN *is greatly agitated.*]

CHRISTIAN.   Cowards! A hundred men
          Against one poet. Oh, to have leave just when
          I've found her. Him. Her. She. He.
          Lignière comes first. Where the hell will he be?

[*He dashes off. The theatre is now full and very impatient.*]

215   SPECTATORS.   Begin! Begin!

[*A man has his wig fished off.*]

FIRST PAGE.   Look at him—bald as a bat!

[*There is joyous laughter, which is suddenly hushed to a silence.* LE BRET *is puzzled.*]

LE BRET.   Why?

[*The* CITIZEN *whispers to him.*]

                        Here? Him? You're sure of that?

CITIZEN.   Would you like a signed certificate?

DRUNKARD.   Mon Dieu—
          Up in that sort of confession-box—Richelieu.

[*He makes the sign of the cross. Richelieu is somewhere high on the fourth wall.*]

FIRST PAGE.　　The cardinal, damn it. Now there's no more fun.

220　**FIRST MARQUIS.**　　Pass me that chair there.

A SPECTATOR.　　　　　　　　　　Quiet, everyone.

[*The baton raps three times. Music.*]

LE BRET.　　He comes on now?

RAGUENEAU.　　　　　　　He starts it off. Very odd.
　　No Cyrano. I've lost my bet.

LE BRET.　　[*fervently but* sotto voce.]　Thank God.

[MONTFLEURY *waddles on, escorted by nymphs. He is grotesquely fat and wears a stylized shepherd's costume with rustic bagpipes under his arm. He graciously acknowledges the applause.*]

SPECTATORS.　　Montfleury—good old Montfleury!

MONTFLEURY.　　Far from the court and city, ah—how good
225　　To breathe the incense of the verdant wood,
　　While cool harmonious breezes seem to say—

VOICE.　　Fat fool, I ordered you to stay away.

[*The* VOICE *utters the line in the same exaggerated stagy manner as* MONTFLEURY. *People look everywhere for the owner of the voice. He is in the auditorium (ours).*]

CUIGY.　　It's him—

LE BRET.　　　　　　God help us all—

VOICE.　　　　　　　　　　Balloon, baboon,
　　Buffoon, for the space of one revolving moon
230　　I ordered you to *rest*. You hesitate?
　　Get off that stage.

SPECTATORS.　　　　　Don't let him intimidate
　　You, Montfleury. Play—continue—carry on—

[*But* MONTFLEURY's *confidence is somewhat diminished.*]

MONTFLEURY.　　Far from the court and city, ah—how—

VOICE.　　　　　　　　　　　　　Good!
　　You see this stick, you clown? I'll plant a wood,
235　　Splinter by splinter, over your rich terrain.

MONTFLEURY.　　Far from the sort and kitty—

VOICE.　　　　　　　　　　Yet again
　　You disobey?

[CYRANO, *first made manifest by voice, then by stick, appears personally, nose flaring, and leaps onto a chair.*]

MONTFLEURY.　[*tremulously.*]　Please help me, gentlemen.

FIRST MARQUIS.　Carry on acting.

CYRANO.　　　　　　　　　　Not for four more weeks.
　　　One word more, and I lambast his shivering cheeks,
240　All four of them.

SECOND MARQUIS.　Enough.

[*Some of the aristocracy rise in protest.*]

CYRANO.　　　　　　　　　　Stay in your stalls,
　　　You vaccine marquises. Your mooing calls
　　　My cane to rummage through your folderols.

DE GUICHE.　This is too much. Continue, Montfleury.

CYRANO.　Discontinue, rather, unless he,
245　Unwilling to retire to sty or trough,
　　　Needs disembowelling and his jowls cut off.
　　　Off, off, you offal. Lug your guts away,
　　　You mortadella. Very well, then—stay,
　　　And I'll remove you slice by slice.

[*MONTFLEURY summons up the remains of his dignity.*]

MONTFLEURY.　　　　　　　　　Monsieur,
250　In insulting me you insult the Tragic Muse.

[*There are some murmurs of agreement and admiration.*]

CYRANO.　[*equably.*]
　　　If the Tragic Muse had the dubious honour, fat sir,
　　　Of your acquaintance, she would not abuse
　　　Her pious duty. Seeing the blubber ooze
　　　Into your collar and your belly round as a clock,
255　She'd kick your buttocks with her tragic sock.

CITIZEN.　[*leading the pit.*]
　　　Carry on, Montfleury—let's hear the play.

CYRANO.　[*kindly.*]
　　　Consider my poor scabbard, please, I pray.
　　　She loves my sword and wants my sword to stay
　　　Inside her. Off that stage! A bleat? A bray?
260　Do any of you have anything to say?

VOICE.   Where's your authority?
                    You go away.
                    We, the majority,
                    Paid for a play.

265 **THE PIT.**   That's right—the play, the play—play the play!

CYRANO.   If I hear this scrannel song once more there'll be
A one-man massacre.

CITIZEN.   You're Samson, eh?

CYRANO.   [*reasonably.*]
Lend me your jawbone, sir, and you'll soon see.

A LADY.   Disgraceful.

CITIZEN.   Shocking.

FIRST MARQUIS.   Scandalous.

FIRST PAGE.   Good fun.

[*The crowd makes animal noises at* CYRANO, *who is unperturbed.*]

270 **CYRANO.**   Silence!

[*He gets it.*]
                    I hereby herewith issue one
            Collective challenge. How about you? Or you?
            Come on, now, who'll be first to breathe his last?
            I'll make a list. To every—er—duellist
            I'll award the funeral honours that are his due.
275   Raise your right hands, all those who wish to die.
            Is it *pudeur* makes you not wish to eye
            My naked blade? Does no one wish to engage
            In a metallic romp? Good. Let me say this: I
            Want something desperately simple—to see the stage
280   Rid of this haemorrhoid, goitre, abscess, tumour.
            And if the flux won't go of its own free will—
            Well, then—the lancet. Buffoon, are you there still?
            Please don't presume too much on my good humour.
            I'll clap my hands three times, you moon of a man.
285   Eclipse yourself on the third clap. Ready? One—

MONTFLEURY.   I, I—

FIRST MARQUIS.   Don't leave.

THE PIT.   Go. Don't go.

MONTFLEURY.   It seems to me—

CYRANO. Two.

MONTFLEURY.   On mature consideration—

CYRANO.   Three.

[MONTFLEURY *disappears with, for his bulk, remarkable speed. There is a storm of roars and whistles.*]

SPECTATORS.   Coward, come back, you coward, coward, come back!

CYRANO. Let him if he dares.

CITIZEN.   Monsieur er Bergerac,
290   This is irregular. I demand a few words
From the head of the company.

SPECTATORS.   Bellerose!

[BELLEROSE *comes on and looks doubtfully at everybody.*]

BELLEROSE.   My lords,
Ladies and gentlemen—one hardly knows what to say.

MUSKETEER. Jodelet!

SPECTATORS.   Jodelet! Bring on Jodelet!

[JODELET *slouches on and looks contemptuously at the spectators. But contempt is part of his act and they enjoy it.*]

JODELET. You flock of muttonheads—

SPECTATORS.   Bravo! Bravo!

JODELET. [*with a strong nasal intonation.*]
295   Let's have no bravos. The distinguished Thespian
Whose paunch you love so much has had to go.

MUSKETEER. He's scared.

JODELET.   Be charitable. Say he's a sick man.

CITIZEN'S SON. [*to* CYRANO.]
But what are your reasons, sir? Why do you show
Such enmity towards Montfleury?

CYRANO. [*courteously.*]   Young ninny,
300   I have two reasons, but let one suffice.
This Montfleury of yours is a deplorable
Mouther, grunter, grimacer, posturer,
Who tears his lines to shivers with a tinny
Voice like a randy cageful of white mice.
305   The second reason? That's my secret.

CITIZEN.   Intolerable
    To deprive us without scruple of a play
    As great as *Clorise*—

CYRANO. [*respectfully.*]
                The work to which you refer,
    You ass, is worth rather less than an ass's bray.
    I silenced it without compunction. Sir.

310   **A PRÉCIEUSE.** Did you hear that?

    ANOTHER.   Really, what can one say?

    ANOTHER. Dear Lord in heaven!

CYRANO. [*gallantly.*]   Ladies of rank and beauty,
    Shiners, enchanters, take it as your duty
    To inspire a poem or epigrammatic witticism,
    But keep your pretty paws off dramatic criticism.

315   **BELLEROSE.** How about all the cash we have to give back?

CYRANO. Bellerose puts us all right. Yes, money matters.
    Let it never be said that Bergerac
    Wished to see Thespis's robe grow full of tatters.

[*He detaches a moneybag from his waist and throws it onto the stage.*]
    Take that. Take off.

JODELET. [*picking up the bag.*]
                If you'll guarantee a sack
320   Of loot like this, I'm ready to guarantee
    To let you shut the theatre every night.

    SPECTATORS. Boo. Boo. Boo.

JODELET.   Even if we
    Get hissed and booed for it.

BELLEROSE.   All right, all right,
    Let's clear the hall.

[*But nobody wants to leave.*]

325   **LE BRET.** It's mad.

CITIZEN.   Yes, mad.
    [*To* CYRANO.]   That very famous actor
    Has His Grace the Duke of Candale as protector.
    Do you have a patron?

CYRANO.   No.

CITIZEN.   No patron?

CYRANO.   No.

CITIZEN.   No patron to protect you with his name?

CYRANO.   No for the third time. I'm protected just the same.
[*He taps his sword.*]
330   *This* is my patroness.

CITIZEN'S SON.   You'll have to go.
You can't stay here in Paris.

CYRANO.   No?

CITIZEN.   Great God,
His Grace—don't you know how long an arm
The duke possesses?

CYRANO.   Less long than mine
When I've screwed on this steel extension rod.

335   CITIZEN.   You honestly think you're able to do him harm?

CYRANO.   It's possible. As for you, please turn you toes
The other way.

CITIZEN.   I beg your—

CYRANO.   Left incline,
Or right. And, thus reoriented, walk.
Or tell me why you're looking at my nose.

[*There is now a terrible expectant silence.*]

340   CITIZEN.   Really, I—

CYRANO.   Unusual, is it? Come on, talk,
Talker, tell me all about it.

CITIZEN.   Really, I
Try not to look at your nose, sir, really—

CYRANO.   Why?
Does it disgust you?

CITIZEN.   No, no, not at all.

CYRANO.   Too lurid, is it? Oversized?

CITIZEN.   It's small,
345   Beautifully small. It's minute—minuscule.

CYRANO.   Compound your insolence with ridicule,
Would you? My nose is small, eh, *small*?

CITIZEN.   Oh God—

CYRANO.   My nose, sir, is enormous. Ignorant clod,
   Cretinous moron, a man ought to be proud,
350 Yes, proud, of having so proud an appendix
   Of flesh and bone to crown his countenance,
   Provided a great nose may be an index
   Of a great soul—affable, kind, endowed
   With wit and liberality and courage
355 And courtesy—like mine, you rat-brained dunce,
   And not like yours, a cup of rancid porridge.
   As for your wretched mug—all that it shows
   Is lack of fire, spunk, of genius, pride,
   Lack of the lyrical and picturesque,
360 Of moral probity—in brief, of nose.
   To fist such nothingness would be grotesque,
   So take a boot instead on your backside.

[*He kicks him. Whimpering, the* CITIZEN *leaves, his* SON, *not too displeased, after him. The aristocrats react unfavourably.*]

DE GUICHE.   He's a bit of a bore.

VALVERT.   A braggart.

DE GUICHE.   Who shall it be,
   My lords?

VALVERT.   [*standing up.*]
     In very bad taste. Only a pig
365 Of a plebeian would sprout a snout like that.

DE GUICHE.   So may we
   Leave it to you?

VALVERT.   Yes, you can leave it to me.

[*So saying, he approaches* CYRANO *with a sneer of great insolence.*]

   That thing of yours is big, what? Very big.

CYRANO.   [*most affably.*]
   Precisely what I was saying.

VALVERT.   Ha!

CYRANO.   Nothing more?
   Just a fatuous smirk? Oh, come, there are fifty-score
370 Varieties of comment you could find
   If you possessed a modicum of mind.
   For instance, there's the frank aggressive kind:
   'If mine achieved that hypertrophic state,

I'd call a surgeon in to amputate.'
375 The friendly: 'It must dip into your cup.
You need a nasal crane to hoist it up.'
The pure descriptive: 'From its size and shape,
I'd say it was a rock, a bluff, a cape—
No, a peninsula—how picturesque!'
380 The curious: 'What's that? A writing desk?'
The gracious: 'Are you fond of birds? How sweet—
A Gothic perch to rest their tiny feet.'
The truculent: 'You a smoker? I suppose
The fumes must gush out fiercely from that nose
385 And people think a chimney is on fire.'
Considerate: 'It will drag you in the mire
Head first, the weight that's concentrated there.
Walk carefully.' The tender hearted swear
They'll have a miniature umbrella made
390 To keep the rain off; or for summer shade.
Then comes the pedant: 'Let me see it, please.
That mythic beast of Aristophanes,
The hippocampocamelelephunt,
Had flesh and bone like that stuck up in front.'
395 Insolent: 'Quite a useful gadget, that.
You hold it high and then hang up your hat.'
Emphatic: 'No fierce wind from near or far,
Save the mistral, could give that nose catarrh.'
Impressed: 'A sign for a perfumery!'
400 Dramatic: 'When it bleeds, it's the Red Sea.'
Lyric: 'Ah, Triton rising from the waters,
Honking his wretched conch at Neptune's daughters.'
Naïve: 'How much to view this monument?'
Speculative: 'Tell me, what's the rent
405 For each or both of those unfurnished flats?'
Rustic: 'Nay, Jarge, that ain't no nose. Why, that's
A giant turnip or a midget marrow.
Let's dig it up and load it on the barrow.'
The warlike: 'Train it on the enemy!'
410 Practical: 'Put that in a lottery
For noses, and it's bound to win first prize.'
And finally, with tragic cries and sighs,
The language finely wrought and deeply felt:
'Oh that this too too solid nose would melt.'
415 That is the sort of thing you could have said

If you, Sir Moron, were a man of letters
Or had an ounce of spunk inside your head.
But you've no letters, have you, save the three
Required for self-description: S.O.T.
420   You have to leave my worsting to your betters,
Or better, who can best you, meaning me.
But be quite sure, you lesser feathered tit,
Even if you possessed the words and wit,
I'd never let you get away with it.

DE GUICHE.   [*apprehensive now.*]
425   Come away, viscount, leave him.

VALVERT.   [*suffocating with rage.*]   Arrogant, base
Nonentity, without even a pair of gloves
To his name, let alone the ribbons and lace
And velvet that a man of breeding loves.

CYRANO.   I'm one of those who wear their elegance
430   Within. To strut around and dance and prance
Got up like a dog's dinner—that's not me.
Less of a fop than you, sir, I may be,
But I'm more wholesome. I have never wandered
Abroad without my insults freshly laundered,
435   Or conscience with the sleep picked from its eye,
Or honour with unragged cuffs. Why, my
Very scruples get a manicure.
When I walk out I like to be quite sure
I smell of nothing but scrubbed liberty
440   And polished independence. You will see
My soul a ramrod as if corseted
And as for ribbons, all I ever did
Brave and adventurous flutters from my clothes.
With spirits high, twirled like mustachios,
445   Among the false and mean I walk about,
And as for spurs, I let the truth clash out.

VALVERT.   [*sputtering.*]   You—

CYRANO.   Gloves, you mentioned gloves. You
have me there.
I have this one left over from a pair—

[*He produces it from his pocket, and a wretched ragged fingerless thing it is.*]

An old, old pair. Its fellow I can't trace.
450   I think I left it in some viscount's face.

VALVERT.   [*throbbing with rage.*]
Cad, villain, clod, flatfooted bloody fool!

[CYRANO, *unmoved, doffs his hat and bows low.*]

CYRANO.   And *I'm* Cyrano Savinien-Hercule
De Bergerac.

[VALVERT *gives him the mandatory glove-blow—on his nose.* CYRANO *remains unmoved.*]

VALVERT.   There.

CYRANO.   Would you be terribly bored
If I composed a poem?

VALVERT.   [*sneering.*]   Poet, eh?

CYRANO.   My lord,
455   I'm thoroughly versed in churning verses out
Even while rattling ironware about.
I'll improvise a ballade.

VALVERT.   [*sneering still.*] A ballade.

CYRANO.   Sorry, my lord, to baffle you with hard
Technical expressions. I'll explain.
460   Three eight-lined stanzas and then one quatrain,
The envoy. Sir, thus my proposal goes:
To fight and at the same time to compose
A ballade of strict classical design,
And then to kill you on the final line.

VALVERT.   [*sure of himself.*]
465   Oh no.

CYRANO.   No? 'Ballade of a Fencing Bout
Between de Bergerac and a Foppish Lout.'

VALVERT.   [*drawing his sword.*]
Well, when you've finished your doggerel recital—

CYRANO.   [*kindly.*]
That was no doggerel. That was the title.
Wait. Let me choose my rhymes—

VALVERT.   Ape.

CYRANO. That's one.

RAGUENEAU. Eel.

470 **CYRANO.** Thank you. Ape rape grape shape feel meal deal seal.
I'm ready.

[*The fighting ballade begins, with* CYRANO *suiting action to words all through it.*]

> I bare my head from crown to nape
> And slowly, leisurely reveal
> The fighting trim beneath my cape,
475 > Then finally I strip my steel.
> A thoroughbred from head to heel,
> Disdainful of the rein or bit,
> Tonight I draw a lyric wheel,
> But, when the poem ends, I hit.
>
480 > Come and be burst, you purple grape,
> Spurt out the juice beneath your peel.
> Gibber, and show, you ribboned ape,
> The fat your folderols conceal.
> Let's ring your bells—a pretty peal!
485 > Is that a fly? I'll see to it.
> Ah, soon you'll feel you blood congeal,
> For, when the poem ends, I hit.
>
> I need a rhyme to hold the shape—
> Gape, fish. I'm going to wind the reel.
490 > My rod is lusting for its rape,
> This sharp tooth slavers for its meal.
> There, let it strike. Ah, did you feel
> The bite? Not yet. The vultures sit
> Until the closing of the deal.
495 > The poem ends, and *then* I hit.

[*He stands solemnly to attention.*]

> Envoy.
> Prince, drop your weapon. Humbly kneel,
> Seek grace from God in requisite
> Repentance. Now—I stamp the seal.
500 > The poem ended—and I hit!

[*He dispatches the viscount neatly.* VALVERT *falls, and his friends gather round him. During the following his body is carried off. There is great excitement and jubilation.*]

CAVALRYMAN.   Superb.

A LADY.   Exquisite.

RAGUENEAU.   Phenomenal.

LE BRET.   Quite mad.

CUIGY.   Heroic.

[A MUSKETEER *not previously noticed comes up to* CYRANO.]

THE MUSKETEER.   Sir, I should be more than glad
        If you'd accept the homage, sir, of one
        Who knows style when he sees it. Oh, *well done.*

[*He goes off.*]

CYRANO.   [*to* LE BRET.]
505   That gentleman—who is he?

LE BRET.   D'Artagnan.
        Come on, let's talk.

CYRANO.   Wait till the mob dies down.
        [*To* BELLEROSE.]
        May we stay here a while?

BELLEROSE.   Of course you can.

[*There is much noise outside.* JODELET *comes in to report.*]

JODELET.   He's being booted and hooted out of town,
        Montfleury.

BELLEROSE.   Tragic stilts to running sandals.
510   *Sic transit.* Lock up, but don't douse the candles.
        We're rehearsing a farce for tomorrow in a
        Quarter of an hour or so. First, though, dinner.

[*The* DOORKEEPER *goes off to do* BELLEROSE'*s bidding, but first he addresses* CYRANO.]

DOORKEEPER.   Will you want dinner?

CYRANO.   Me? No.

LE BRET.   And why not?

CYRANO.   No money.

LE BRET.   I see. Every sou you'd got—

515   CYRANO.   Oh, shall we say:
        One glorious day
        Of life for a month's pay.

LE BRET.   And how will you live the month out?

CYRANO.   I don't know.

LE BRET.   A stupid act.

CYRANO.   A marvellous gesture, though.

[*The* FOODSELLER *has been hovering with her cart of comestibles.*]

520   FOODSELLER.   Pardon, sir, I couldn't help but hear.
          You mustn't starve. Take something. Please.

CYRANO.   My dear,
          The pride of a Gascon, you must understand,
          Forbids my taking from your lily hand
          The tiniest morsel. But rather than rebuff
525   Such kindness—just a grape—one is enough—
          A glass of water. Half a biscuit.

LE BRET.   This
          Is stupid.

FOODSELLER.   Nothing more?

CYRANO.   Your hand to kiss.

[*He salutes her courteously.*]

FOODSELLER.   Thank you, sir. Goodnight.

[*She trips off queenily.* CYRANO *spreads his handkerchief on a bench and sits before it with a gourmet's seriousness. He and* LE BRET *are now quite alone.*]

CYRANO.   Well now, we're able
          To talk at last. Dinner is on the table—
530   Main course, a drink, dessert. Strangely, I find
          I've quite an appetite. What's on your mind?

LE BRET.   Listen. These jingling fops with their bellicose airs
          Are starting to twist and torture your ideas
          Of gentlemanly behaviour. Ask anyone
535   Of sense what they think of these—carryings on.

CYRANO.   [*eating.*]
          Delicious.

LE BRET.   The cardinal—

CYRANO.   He was here?

LE BRET.   Richelieu
          Is bound to find that sort of thing—

CYRANO.   *Vieux jeu.*

LE BRET.   Have some sense.

CYRANO.   He's an author himself. He won't rage
To see someone else's play kicked off the stage.

540   LE BRET.   But can't you understand? Your enemies
Are multiplying.

CYRANO.   The latest figure is . . . ?

LE BRET.   Excluding women, forty-eight, by my count.

CYRANO.   Enumerate.

LE BRET.   Oh, Montfleury, the viscount—
His relicts, I mean—the author's friends, that frightful
545   De Guiche, of course, the Academy—

CYRANO.   Delightful.

LE BRET.   This life of yours—where will it lead you to?
What system is it based on?

CYRANO.   Bumbling through
In aimless complication, forced to play
Too many parts—that was my old way.
550   But now—

LE BRET.   What?

CYRANO.   I'm going to take the simplest
Approach to life of all, simplest and best.
Best is the word. I've decided to excel
In everything.

LE BRET.   [*sighing.*]
                         I let that pass. Now tell
Me, please, the thing I really want to know—
555   Your true reason, *true*, mind, for this show
Of hate for Montfleury.

CYRANO.   [*with bitter detestation.*]
                              That paunch, that maw,
Too fat to scratch his navel with his paw,
Believes he's a sweet danger to the ladies.
Why, even when mouthing tragedy, he's made his
560   Frog's eyes into sheep's eyes of fat lust.
I've seen him, and I've choked down my disgust.
Until, one night, one victim that he chose—
Ugh, a slug slithering over a white rose—
One lady . . .

LE BRET.   Yes?

CYRANO.   I was in love with. No, God knows,
565   I *am* in love with—

LE BRET.   [*greatly surprised.*]
                        But you never said one word.
       How could he know, how could anyone?

CYRANO.   Absurd,
       Isn't it? This nose precedes me everywhere,
       A quarter of an hour in front, to say 'Beware:
       Don't love Cyrano' to even the ugliest.
570   And Cyrano now has to love the best,
       The brightest, bravest, wittiest, the most
       Beautiful.

LE BRET.   Beautiful?

CYRANO.   France cannot boast,
       Nor Europe, nor all territories beyond,
       A girl more lissom, gossamer-fine, more blonde—

575   **LE BRET.**   Blonde? My God, who is this woman?

[CYRANO, *with no deliberate intention, now falls into the pattern of a Petrarchan sonnet, as though this lady were Laura.*]

CYRANO.   She's
       A mortal danger without knowing it,
       Undreamed-of-in-her-own-dreams exquisite,
       A roseleaf ambush where love lurks to seize
       The unwary heart. The unwary eye that sees
580   Her smile sees pearled perfection. She can knit
       Grace from a twine of air. The heavens sit
       In every gesture. Of divinities
       She's most divine. O Venus, amorous queen,
       You never stepped into your shell; Dian—
585   You never glided through the summer's green
       As *she* steps into her chair and then is seen
       Gliding through dirty Paris—

LE BRET.   There's no ban
       On uttering her name—your cousin's name?

CYRANO.   It rhymes, and that's enough. Let not the shame
590   Of the dusty air besmirch it—

LE BRET.   Oh—absurd.

This is the finest news I ever heard.
You love her? Fine—so go and tell her so.
Tonight you're covered in a golden glow
Of glory in her eyes.

CYRANO.   This—gross protuberance.
595   Look at it, and tell me what exuberance
Of hope can swell the rest of me. I'm under
No illusion. Oh, sometimes, bemused by the wonder
Of a blue evening, a garden of lilac and rose,
Letting this wretched devil of a nose
600   Breathe in the perfume, I follow with my eye—
Under that silver glory in the sky—
Some woman on the arm of a cavalier,
And dream that I too could be strolling there,
With such a girl on *my* arm, under the moon.
605   My heart lifts, I forget my curse, but soon,
Suddenly, I perceive what kills it all—
My profile shadowed on the garden wall.

LE BRET.   [*with pity.*]
My friend—

CYRANO.   My friend, why should providence allot
Such ugliness, such loneliness?

LE BRET.   You're not
610   *Crying?*

CYRANO.   Oh, never, never that. To see
A long tear straggling along this nose would be
Intolerably ugly. I wouldn't permit
A crystal tear fraught with such exquisite
Limpidity to be defiled by my
615   Gross snout. Tears are sublime things, and I,
Wedding a nymph to a rhinoceros,
Would render the sublime ridiculous.

[*But this speech, rendered rapidly and unrhetorically, is a kind of handkerchief.*]

LE BRET.   All right, not crying, but still sad. Yet love
Is an imponderable, not a matter of—
620   Well, nasal mensuration. March right in.
If love, as they say, is a lottery, you can—

CYRANO.   Argh.
I love Cleopatra. Have I Antony's

Glamour and glow and glory? And if she's
Hero, though I can swim, I'm no Leander.
625   A new Roxane needs a new Alexander,
And I'm the Great in only one respect.
Helen of Paris—whom can she select
But Paris of Paris? I'm not he.

LE BRET.   But your wit,
Your courage—they can earn love. Surely it
630   Was proved just now. The girl who offered you
Food—did her eyes show hate, revulsion?

CYRANO.   [*doubtfully.*]   True.

LE BRET.   Well, then—I saw her face, Roxane's, tonight
During your duel. It was ghastly white.
That skill, that courage got the girl. You're half-
635   Way there. Now dare to speak.

CYRANO.   So she can laugh
At *this*? Why, man, there's nothing that I fear
More in this world—

[*During the above, the DOORKEEPER has made a quiet entrance.*]

DOORKEEPER.   Monsieur, there's someone here
Who'd like a word with you.

[*They see who it is.*]

CYRANO.   Heavens, her chaperone.

[*Roxane's DUENNA comes up to them, curtsies, and speaks in prose.*]

DUENNA.   I have a message. My lady says she'd be glad if
640   her brave cousin, as she puts it, would be good enough to
meet her in private, as she puts it.

CYRANO.   [*astonished.*]   She wants to meet me?

DUENNA.   She has something to say to you, so she says to
me. She's going to early mass tomorrow. Saint-Roch. She
645   wants to know where she can see you afterwards.

CYRANO.   Oh, heavens, let me think—

DUENNA.   Where?

CYRANO.   I'm thinking where. Where? At the shop of
Monsieur Ragueneau the pastrycook.

650   **DUENNA.**   Where?

CYRANO.   At the shop of—in the rue Saint-Honoré.

DUENNA.   Seven o'clock. She'll be there.

CYRANO.   I'll be there.

DUENNA.   I'll be with her. Goodnight.

[*She curtsies and is off.* LE BRET *and* CYRANO *look at each other in joy.*]

655   CYRANO.   Me—she wants to see *me*.

LE BRET.   So it's goodbye
    To misery?

CYRANO.   Whatever she wants, it means that I
    At least exist for her—

LE BRET.   So now—an accession of calm?

CYRANO.   Calm? With ten hearts beating within, each arm
    As muscular as twenty? My arteries thud
660   With thunder, lightning's jagging through my blood.
    I need an army meet for my defiance.
    So take away your dwarfs—bring on your giants!

[*During the above, the theatrical company, in commedia dell'arte costumes, have been assembling on the stage.*]

BELLEROSE.   Quiet down there, we're rehearsing.

CYRANO.   [*laughing.*]   And we're off.

[*They march towards the door, but this opens, and* CUIGY *and* BRISSAILLE *half carry in the dead-drunk* LIGNIÈRE.]

CUIGY.   Thank God you're here.

CYRANO.   What the devil—

BRISSAILLE.   Devil enough,
665   This one.

CYRANO.   What's the trouble?

[LIGNIÈRE, *thick-voiced, tremulously proffers a tattered piece of paper.* CYRANO *reads what is on it.*]

LIGNIÈRE.   I got this note.
    A hundred men—because of a song I wrote—
    I daren't go home—you hear—a hundred men—
    Going to get me—armed, the lot of them—when
    I go through the Porte de Nesle—my way home. Let me
670   Stay in your place—hundred men—going to get me.

CYRANO. [*with restrained joy.*]
    A hundred men? Tonight you lay your head
    On your own pillow.

LIGNIÈRE.   But—

CYRANO.   I'll turn down your bed
    Myself. I swear it. Now, get off your knees
    And take that lantern.

[*He means one of the enclosed candles used for lighting the theatre,* LIGNIÈRE *shakily obeys.* CYRANO *addresses the others.*]

                      You, the witnesses
675   Of what I intend to do, come too, but please
    Keep a safe distance.

CUIGY.   You mean—you're going to fight
    One hundred men?

CYRANO.   Certainly. Tonight
    Less than a hundred would be far too few.

[*The* ACTORS *and* ACTRESSES, *intrigued, have come down from the stage.*]

LE BRET.   [*indicating* LIGNIÈRE.]
    But why protect this—?

CYRANO.   I expected you,
680   Captain, to raise objections.

LE BRET.   Drunken sot?

CYRANO.   This drunken sot, this claret butt, this pot
    Of mountain dew, once did a thing as pretty
    As ever I saw. It happened here, in the city.
    Mass had just ended. He saw a girl he loved
685   Dip in the holy water font. He shoved
    His whole head in and drank the blessed lot.

ACTRESS.   A lovely thing to do.

CYRANO.   Yes, was it not?
    Sot!

[*He tousles* LIGNIÈRE's *hair affectionately and claps a hat on it.*]

ACTRESS.   But a hundred men against one poor
    Poet—why?

CYRANO.   Let's march. When I make for
690   The enemy, don't help, no matter what
    The danger.

ANOTHER ACTRESS. I must come and see.

CYRANO.   Why not?
  All of you! Make with mad and motley charm a
  Blend of Italian farce and Spanish drama.
  Bring silver music, so the noisy scene
695 Both thuds and jingles—like a tambourine.

ACTRESSES.   Wonderful—quick, a cloak—I need a hood.

CYRANO.   Gentlemen of the orchestra, will you . . . ? Good.

[*He starts getting his retinue in line.*]

  Gentlemen first, the ladies next, but some
  Twenty paces in the van I come
700 Alone, save for this triple-waving plume,
  This proud panache. Nobody must presume
  To aid me in this fight—*my* fight, *my* war.
  One, two, three—doorman, open up the door.

[*The* DOORKEEPER *opens up the fourth wall. Nocturnal music sounds from the heavens.*]

  Ah, Paris, swimming through nocturnal mist,
705 The rooftops draped in azure, shyly kissed
  By an uncertain moon—proscenium
  All dressed and ready for the scene to come.
  Below, threading the fog, a silver skein,
  Or like a magic mirror, breathes the Seine,
710 Trembling, compact of myth and mystery—
  You're going to see now what you're going to see.
  To the Porte de Nesle!

EVERYBODY.   To the Porte de—

[CYRANO *stops them with an upheld hand and answers a question already asked.*]

CYRANO.   There was
  A question: why do five-score enemies
  Seek to stick five-score daggers in the back
715 Of one poor poet? Answer: it's because
  They know this poor defenceless rhymer is
  A friend of Cyrano de Bergerac!
  To the Porte de Nesle!

EVERYBODY.   To the Porte de Nesle!
[*Music. Off they go.*]

[CURTAIN.]

Act 2

Ragueneau's shop

[*It is the following morning, very early, dawn indeed.* RAGUENEAU'S *rôtisserie already exudes heartening aromas of things aroast and abake.* RAGUENEAU *himself sits at a table counting off poetic feet on his fingers, between two of which is a quill pen. Scrawled paper is before him.* COOKS *emerge from the kitchen bearing dishes which they place upon a counter. They announce what the dishes are.*]

FIRST COOK.   Fruit flan.

SECOND COOK.   Terrine of beef.

THIRD COOK.   Pork pâté.

FOURTH COOK.   Tarts.

[*Having set down their trays, they return to the kitchen.* RAGUENEAU *sighs.*]

RAGUENEAU.   Smelling hot fat, my frigid muse departs.
The dawn is silvering each casserole,
So lock the god of poetry in your soul.
5   Quit cool Parnassus for this nether fire.
The ovens beckon. *Au revoir*, my lyre.

[*Some of the baking and roasting proceeds in the back part of the shop itself.* RAGUENEAU *superintends the work. He addresses a baker.*]

These lumps are badly placed. You have to fix
The caesura there—between the hemistichs.
[*To one working on a piecrust.*]
This dome of pastry needs a cupola.
[*To one who is fixing poultry on spits.*]
10   You—alternate the modest fowl and the
Proud turkey like the long verse and the short.
Thus you compose upon the spit a sort
Of browning stanza, a roast symmetry.

[*An* APPRENTICE *brings in a pastry confection in the shape of a lyre.* RAGUENEAU *is deeply touched.*]

APPRENTICE.   How do you like it, sir?

RAGUENEAU.   You thought of me.
15   Charming.

APPRENTICE.   *Brioche*. The strings here are a little—

RAGUENEAU.   Brittle?

APPRENTICE.   Sugar.

RAGUENEAU.   At last a synthesis
Of poetry and pastry. Good. Drink this.

[*He gives the* APPRENTICE *money. But* LISE, RAGUENEAU'*s wife, comes in. She carries paper bags to give him. On her feet shoe-dusters are affixed for polishing the floor. She is prettyish, dumpy, flirtatious, a shrew.*]

Here comes your mistress. Hide the money, quick.
[*Ingratiatingly.*]
How do you like it, dear—this thing?

LISE.   Ridic-
20   Ulous.

RAGUENEAU.   Ulous. Paper bags? Good. Good
God, woman, this is poetry—how could
You desecrate—dismember my friends' verse?
Blasphemy, sacrilege—ah, no, it's worse—
It's the Bacchantes ripping Orpheus again.

25   LISE.   What else are those rotten scribbles fit for, then?
They'll do a job now, and that's fit and proper.

RAGUENEAU.   [*weightily.*]
Ant—you're insulting the divine grasshopper.

LISE.   A rotten lot—all ragged shirts and pants—
Before you met them you never called me ants
30   And back ants.

RAGUENEAU.   But—to do *that*, with *those*!
It makes me wonder what you'd do with prose.

[*Scratching his bottom, shaking his head, he goes towards the counter. Two* CHILDREN *enter.*]

RAGUENEAU.   Yes, my pretties?

FIRST CHILD.   Three pies.

RAGUENEAU. How about these—
All hot and brown?

SECOND CHILD. Please will you wrap them, please?

RAGUENEAU. Ah God, my poets' poems. Heavens, this is
35 Penelope's epistle to Ulysses.
Not that. 'The god Apollo, blond and bright . . .'
Not that one either.

LISE. [pausing in her dusting.]
Don't keep the customers waiting.

RAGUENEAU. 'Sonnet to Phyllis'—sacrilege. Oh, all right.

[She turns her back. He addresses the CHILDREN earnestly in a whisper.]

Don't go away. Come back. Here—give it me,
40 And I'll let you have six pies instead of three.

[The CHILDREN happily run off with six pies unwrapped. RAGUENEAU unhappily smooths out the defiled poem.]

RAGUENEAU. 'O glorious Phyllis'—what an inglorious shame:
Some cooking fat has smeared that lovely name.

[CYRANO enters impetuously.]

CYRANO. What time is it?

RAGUENEAU. Six o'clock.

CYRANO. Another hour.

RAGUENEAU. [coming towards him.]
Felicitations. Ah—such skill, such power.
45 I saw it all.

CYRANO. Saw what all?

RAGUENEAU. Your duel in rhyme.

LISE. He talks about it all the blessed time.

CYRANO. Oh that—

RAGUENEAU. 'The poem ended—and I hit.'
Such a synthesis of steel and style—such tricks,
Such tropes—

CYRANO. The time?

RAGUENEAU. Thirty seconds past six.

[LISE comes towards him in her dusting dance and, with woman's sharpness, sees that he has a slash on his hand.]

50　　Rhyme and rapier—wonderful. 'The poem ended—
　　　And I—

LISE.　　　　Ah, shut up. Here you—where and when did
　　You get that?

CYRANO.　　　Only a scratch.

LISE.　　　　　　　　　Patch it, get some ointment.

CYRANO.　　It's nothing, I tell you. Listen, I have an appointment
　　Here, soon. Leave us alone, will you?

55　RAGUENEAU.　　Alone? I can't. You see, my poets are due—

LISE.　　That's right. For their first meal of the day.

CYRANO.　　When I give you the signal, get them away.
　　The time?

RAGUENEAU.　　Six and ninety seconds.

CYRANO.　　　　　　　　　—To write it on.
　　Ah.

[He sits at RAGUENEAU's table. He examines a poetic draft and winces. He takes a clean sheet of paper. He looks for a pen. RAGUENEAU gives him one from behind his ear.]

RAGUENEAU.　　Try this. It once belonged to a swan.

[CYRANO nods his thanks and takes it. He prepares to write. The MUSKETEER we saw at the theatre comes in loudly and confidently. He goes straight to LISE.]

60　MUSKETEER.　　Morning!

CYRANO.　　　　　　　　What's that?

RAGUENEAU.　[resignedly.]　　　　A sort of friend of my wife.
　　Very fierce. So he tells me.

CYRANO.　　　　　　　Right. Write.
　　Fold. Give it her. Transform my life.
　　The time?

RAGUENEAU.　　Two minutes past.

CYRANO.　　　　　　　　Of all within
　　I have of words, just one. Oh, let's begin.
65　Letter written a hundred times in my heart—
　　It's ready enough. Why hesitate to start?
　　My soul on paper—hope unmarked by doubt.
　　A simple matter of copying it out.

[*He writes. Ragueneau's* POET FRIENDS, *having cast their wretched shadows on the window, come in, filthy, ragged, probably untalented. There are five of them.*]

LISE.   Here comes the gorgers.

[*They ignore* LISE *and greet* RAGUENEAU *extravagantly.*]

FIRST POET.   *Confrère!*

SECOND POET   *Cher confrère!*

70   THIRD POET.   Lord of the heavenly roast.

FOURTH POET.   [*sniffing.*]   How good the air
     Smells in thy dwelling.

FIFTH POET.   Phoebus of the flans.

FIRST POET.   Apollo of the *poulet.*

RAGUENEAU.   They make a man's
     Heart lift on very entrance.

[*They start eating, but only behind each other's backs. They have a certain rough delicacy.*]

FIRST POET.   Sorry we're late.
     We got held up by the crowd at the Porte de Nesle.

75   SECOND POET.   Villainous-looking corpses head to tail
     Laid in the morning mud. I counted eight.

CYRANO.   [*without looking up.*]
     I made it seven.

RAGUENEAU.   [*to* CYRANO.]
                    Do you happen to know
     Who the hero of this massacre happens to be?

CYRANO.   [*writing.*]   Me? No?

THIRD POET.   He split from the nave to the chaps
80   These eight—or seven—and sent off ninety-three—
     Or two—screaming like cats.

LISE.   [*to the* MUSKETEER.]   Do *you* know?

MUSKETEER.   [*twirling his moustache.*]   Perhaps.

CYRANO.   [*writing.*]   *Je vous aime . . .*

SECOND POET.   Blood guts brains swords pikes—

CYRANO.   [*writing.*]   *Vos yeux . . .*

FIRST POET.   Hats and cloaks as far as the Quai des Orfèvres—

SECOND POET.   He must be the devil himself—

CYRANO.   *Vos lèvres.*

85   **THIRD POET.**   A giant, a monster, without one particle of—

CYRANO.   'Fear makes me tremble when I look at you.'

FOURTH POET.   Written any poems lately, Ragueneau?

CYRANO.   [*finishing his letter.*]   That will do.
No signature. End, as begin, with love.
Then give it to her—

RAGUENEAU.   I've done this little thing—
90   A recipe in verse.

[*The* POETS, *anticipating their reward for listening, fall to more openly.*]

FIRST POET.   [*munching.*]
We're all ears.

SECOND POET.   [*indistinctly.*]   Sing.

THIRD POET.   Feed us, I mean Phoebus, flash lyric fire.

[POETS *4 and 5 are now working, from opposite ends, on the lyre-shaped confectionary.*]

FOURTH POET.   For the first time in history, the lyre
Sustains the poet.

FIRST POET [*to* SECOND POET.]
Having a good breakfast?

SECOND POET.   Dinner
Of the night before last.

RAGUENEAU.   Gentlemen, I'll begin. 'A
95   Recipe for Making Almond Tarts.'

[*The* POETS *applaud as if they already heard the poem.* RAGUENEAU *gently rebukes them.*]

That is the title. *Now* the poem starts.

Poised on steady legs,
First your poet begs
Several eggs.
100   Froth them to a mousse,
And then introduce
Lemon juice.
Shimmering like silk,
Aromatic milk

105	Of almonds will c—
	ome next, and next prepare
	Pastry light as air
	To coat with care
	Each pretty pastry mould,
110	Which sweetly will enfold
	The liquid gold.
	Smile, a father, fond.
	Wave your fiery wand,
	Bake till blond.
115	Melting mouths and hearts,
	Mmmmmm, saliva starts—
	Almond tarts.

POETS. Exquisite! Delicious!

FIRST POET. [*belching.*] Waaaaargh.

CYRANO. That ninth line's rough.

[*RAGUENEAU, counting on his fingers, nods ruefully.*]

RAGUENEAU. Will c—ome.

CYRANO. Don't you see how they stuff and stuff?

120 **RAGUENEAU.** They're welc—ome. Yes, I see it well enough,
But I don't look. Looking would put them off.
Don't worry about me. I get a double treat:
They listen, but, better than that, they eat.
They need to.

CYRANO. [*affectionately punching him.*]
You're a good man, Ragueneau.

[*RAGUENEAU talks with his friends about prosody. CYRANO goes over to LISE, who leaves her MUSKETEER to go over to him.*]

125 Madame, a word.

LISE. [*truculently.*] What about?

CYRANO. Keep it low.
Tell me, is he laying siege, this musketeer?

LISE. Nobody goes too far with me. All I do
Is shoot them down with my eyes.

CYRANO. Indeed? Those two

Blue conquerors look strangely conquered to me.
130   They're showing their white flags.

LISE.   Now you look here—

CYRANO.   Your generous-hearted husband happens to be
        A friend of mine. And I will not let you
        Ridicule him, cuckold him, the two—
        Ridicuckold—

LISE.   If you think that—

CYRANO.   I do.

[*He moves nearer to the* MUSKETEER *and speaks more loudly.*]

135   A word to the wise, as the saying goes,
        Or—if your Latin isn't rusty too—

[*He indicates the* MUSKETEER's *scabbarded sword.*]

        Verb. sap.

[*He marches back towards* RAGUENEAU.]

    LISE.   [*enraged.*]
                Give him a slap on his nose.

    MUSKETEER.   His nose, yes, his nose—

[*But* CYRANO *turns and quells him with a look. The* MUSKETEER *doffs his hat and smiles ingratiatingly.*]

                                    Pardon me.
            I was just—

[*But* CYRANO's *look is enough to send him scuttling off to, presumably, the living quarters of the premises.* LISE, *blazing, follows him.* CYRANO *sees a couple of shadows on the window. He indicates to* RAGUENEAU *that the shop be cleared.*]

    CYRANO.   Psst.

    RAGUENEAU.   [*to the* POETS.]
                Let's go inside. It will be
140   Less distracting—for the Muse, that is.

    FIRST POET.   [*with rare candour.*]
            To hell with the Muse. Food first.

    SECOND POET.   [*shocked.*]   Blasphemies.

[*But he is the first to take a tray of cakes and to follow* RAGUENEAU. CYRANO *is alone.*]

CYRANO.   So out this letter comes if I can see
The faintest wisp of hope—

[*ROXANE, masked, enters with her DUENNA. To the latter CYRANO at once addresses himself.*]

                                        Madame, a quick
Word—

DUENNA.   Two if you like, monsieur.

CYRANO.   Are you
145   By way of being a gourmande?

DUENNA.   I can do
The gourmandizing act until I'm sick.

CYRANO.   Good. I take a Pindaric ode or two—

DUENNA.   Eh?

CYRANO.   Making the subject-matter chocolate éclairs.

[*He suits actions to words.*]

DUENNA.   Ah!

CYRANO.   Do you like cream puffs?

DUENNA.   So long as there's
150   More cream than puff.

CYRANO.   This ode looks puffy enough.
As for this epic on a lovesick soul—
It's deep enough, I think, for a whole jam roll.
Go and commune, madame, with the rising sun.
Masticate thoroughly. Don't come back till you're done.

[*The DUENNA is not sure whether she is doing the right thing. Greed defeats duty. She goes out cake-laden. CYRANO and ROXANE are alone.*]

155   **CYRANO.**   May that one hour of all the hours be blessed
When you at last remembered I exist
And came to tell me—what?

ROXANE.   First I must
Thank you for last night. That wretch—that fop
You—punctured—his patron is eaten up
160   With what he calls love—

CYRANO.   De Guiche?

ROXANE.   De Guiche proposed
That I should marry—

CYRANO.   A blasphemous disguise
     For his own—I see. That's one bad chapter closed.
     I fought not for my nose but your bright eyes.

ROXANE.   The other thing is—I daren't mention it yet.
165   I must see you first as you were—the—almost brother
     You used to be when we were children together
     Playing in the park, by the lake—

CYRANO.   How can I forget
     The summers that you spent at Bergerac?

ROXANE.   When your swords were bulrushes.

CYRANO.   And the golden hair
170   Of your doll was cornsilk.

ROXANE.   Beanfields in the air,
     Green plums and perpetual playtime.

CYRANO.   Puppies and
     Mulberries. Heavens, how I'm taken back.

ROXANE.   To when my wish was always your command.

CYRANO.   Short-skirted Roxane. You used to be Madeleine.

175   ROXANE. Was I pretty?

CYRANO.   You were never exactly plain.

ROXANE.   I remember—you'd climb a tree and hurt your hand,
     And come running to me. And then I'd play
     The mother, and all gruff and grown-up I'd say:
     'How on earth did you manage to—?'

[*She has taken his hand. That scratch looks more serious than* CYRANO *said. He
tries to snatch it away but she grasps it firmly.*]

                                        Oh, no. How
180   On earth? Let me see it. *Let me see*—Oh, even now,
     At your age!

CYRANO.   A bit of rather rough play
     With some of the big boys, down by the Porte de Nesle.

ROXANE.   Give it to me.

[*She dips her handkerchief in a jug of something—probably wine. She cleans the
wound.*]

CYRANO.   Yes, mama.

ROXANE. Playing, indeed. Tell
Me—how many of these big boys were there?

CYRANO. Oh, about
185   A hundred.

[*She does not at first take this in.*]

ROXANE. About a hundred. *A hundred!* Out
With your story—come now—

CYRANO. Out with yours—
If it *is* a story. If you dare tell it—yet.

ROXANE. I do dare. How easily one conjures
The scent of the past. I'm breathing it,
190   And you and I are home again. So listen now.
I'm in love with someone.

CYRANO. Ah.

ROXANE. With someone who
Doesn't know, doesn't suspect.

CYRANO. Ah.

ROXANE. Not yet, anyway.

CYRANO. Ah.

ROXANE. But he will know. Soon.

CYRANO. Ah.

ROXANE. He loves me too,
But so far from a distance, timidly,
195   Poor boy, too scared to speak.

CYRANO. Ah.

ROXANE. Can you say
Nothing but 'Ah'?

CYRANO. Ah.

ROXANE. Give me back your hand.
How hot it is—feverish. But I see
Love trembling on his lip.

CYRANO. Ah.

ROXANE. He's a soldier, and,
More than that, he's in your regiment.

200 **CYRANO.** Ah.

ROXANE.   More than that, even, he's in your company.

CYRANO. Ah.

ROXANE.   And such a man—intelligent,
Young, brave, beautiful.

CYRANO. [*pale, rising.*]   Beautiful?

ROXANE. Whatever's the matter?

CYRANO.   Nothing. Just this fool
Of a scratch I got from the big boys.

[*He smiles.*]

ROXANE.   Anyway,
205   I love him. All that remains for me to say
Is that I've only seen him at the theatre.

CYRANO.   Never met?
Never spoken?

ROXANE.   Only with our eyes.

CYRANO.   Then how can you
Know?

ROXANE.   Oh, you know how it is. People talk—
In the Place Royale—gossip as they walk
210   Under the lime trees.

CYRANO.   He's in the Guards, you say.
His name?

ROXANE.   Baron Christian de Neuvillette.

CYRANO.   He's not in the Guards.

ROXANE.   Oh yes, he is, as from today—
Under Captain Carbon de Castel-Jaloux.

CYRANO.   So soon, so fast, the knife can pierce our hearts.
215   My poor dear child—

[*Roxane's DUENNA comes blithely in.*]

DUENNA.   Monsieur de Bergerac,
I've eaten every single one of those tarts.

CYRANO.   Good. Now read the wrappers, front and back.

[*She goes out again, shrugging.*]

My dear sweet child—think—consider—you

Who love fine words, eloquence, elegance—
220   He may be a fool, a savage—

ROXANE.   Oh, but his
Curls are the curls of a Greek god.

CYRANO.   There's a chance
That his brains may be curly too.

ROXANE.   That can't be true.
My woman's instincts tell me otherwise.

CYRANO.   Those instincts often tell the biggest lies.
225   Suppose he's a boor, a bore—what will you do?

ROXANE.   [with touching simplicity.]
Well, then, I suppose I shall have to die.

CYRANO.   And so—you brought me here to tell me this.
Perhaps you'd be good enough to tell me why.

ROXANE.   Yesterday someone said—oh, it frightens me—
230   Somebody said that all your company
Are Gascons.

CYRANO.   Yes, all Gascons. Ah, I see!
It's a matter of our fiery Gascon pride
To rip up any greenhorn from outside
Who gets inside. Is that what you heard?

ROXANE.   I'm scared
235   For him.

CYRANO.   [between his teeth.]
              Not without cause.

ROXANE.   But you, who dared
So much last night—that brute, those brutes—everyone
Is so scared of you—I thought—

CYRANO.   Your Christian
Shall not be thrown to the lions.

ROXANE.   For our friendship's sake
You'll protect him? Defend him? You'll make
240   Him your friend?

CYRANO.   There's nothing finer than
Friendship.

ROXANE.   Promise.

CYRANO.   I promise.

ROXANE. Don't let anyone
Fight duels with him.

CYRANO. God forbid.

ROXANE. [*fervently.*] Oh, Cyrano,
I love you. Tell me everything about last night
Some time, won't you? Now I have to go.
245 Oh, how I love you. Oh, and tell him to write.

CYRANO. Yes, yes.

ROXANE. Don't forget now. Just think—a hundred men
Against my boy of the bulrush sword. Ah, when
There's time you must tell me. We're friends, aren't we?

CYRANO. Yes, yes.

ROXANE. Tell him to write. You and a hundred men.
250 Such courage.

[*Leaving, she blows him a kiss. He stands frozen.*]

CYRANO. I've done better than that since then.

[*Silence. The door opens. Captain* CARBON DE CASTEL-JALOUX *comes in, a handsome, brave, rather conventional officer.*]

CARBON. May I come in?

CYRANO. Yes, yes, you love me.

CARBON. Eh?

[CYRANO *comes to.*]

CYRANO. Captain.

CARBON. [*patting him on the back.*]
We've heard the story, but we want it from you.
There are thirty cadets of the Guards all ready to
Get you drunk, in the tavern across the way.
255 Come on.

CYRANO. I'd rather not.

[CARBON *shrugs and goes to the door. He shouts. At the same time* RAGUENEAU *comes in from the kitchen.*]

CARBON. Hey there! Hey!
Our hero's suffering from a sort of crapula—
Too much blood. Come over.

[*He strides back to* CYRANO, *smiling.*]

Talk about popular—

[*The* CADETS *enter noisily. They express delight, in the Gascon dialect, at seeing* CYRANO.]

      CADETS.   *Mille dioux! Capdedious! Mordious! Pocapdedious!*

      RAGUENEAU.   You're Gascons, gentlemen, are you—all of you?

260   **FIRST CADET.**   Well done.

      CYRANO.   [*formally.*]   Baron.

      SECOND CADET.   First class.

      CYRANO.   Baron.

      THIRD CADET.   Bravo!

      CYRANO.   Baron.

      FOURTH CADET.   Let me kiss you.

      FIFTH CADET.   Me too.

      CYRANO.   Barons—no!

      RAGUENEAU.   And you're all barons too?

      FIRST CADET.   Baronially born.
        You could build a tower with our coronets, monsieur.

      SECOND CADET.   But first you'd have to get them out of pawn.

[*During the above* LE BRET *enters. He strides up to his friend.*]

265   **LE BRET.**   Cyrano, the whole of Paris is here,
        Looking for you—a delirious crowd behind me,
        Led by the ones you led along last night.

      CYRANO.   I trust you didn't say where they could find me.

      LE BRET.   I did.

[*A* CITIZEN *comes in and leaves the door open.*]

      CITIZEN.   See—carriages—the street's packed tight.

270   **LE BRET.**   How about Roxane?

      CYRANO.   Quiet!

[*A crowd comes in, jubilant.*]

      CROWD.   Cyrano!

      RAGUENEAU.   [*with delight.*]   My shop
        Is invaded. They'll smash everything up.
        Magnificent!

[*Members of the crowd fawn on* CYRANO, *maul him, seek to embrace him.*]

    CROWD.   My friend—my friend—my friend—

    CYRANO.   I never knew
    I had so many friends.

    LE BRET.   Success at last.

[CYRANO *looks bitterly at him. A foppish* MARQUIS *comes up and tries to embrace the hero.*]

275   MARQUIS.   My dear—

    CYRANO.   Too dear for customers like you
    To handle.

[*He is unhandled. The* MARQUIS *is affronted, but another one comes up to* CYRANO *with large enthusiasm, handling him.*]

    OTHER MARQUIS.
                 The ladies in my carriage, sir, have just
    Expressed a desire to meet you. Allow me to
    Present you to them.

[*He goes ahead, confident that* CYRANO *will follow.*]

    CYRANO.   Certainly.
    But first, sir, who'll present *you* to *me*?

280   LE BRET.   What the—

[*A self-important* MAN OF LETTERS *enters.*]

    CYRANO.   Quiet!

    MAN OF LETTERS.   I'd like some details—

    CYRANO.   No!

    LE BRET.   Oh, come now, this is Théophraste Renaudot,
    Founder of the *Gazette.* Up-to-the-minute
    News is his line. There's a big future in it,
    Or so they tell me.

[RENAUDOT *retires hurt. His place is taken by a* POET—*a decently dressed one, not one of* RAGUENEAU'S *wretched friends.*]

    POET.   I'd like your permission,
285   Sir, to write a celebratory composition—
    An acrostic on your name.

    CYRANO.   I'll do it better.
    I'll do it now. You can call out each letter
    And I can do the rest. Come on, then—go!

POET. See—

CYRANO.   these vassals of emotion.

290 **POET.** Why—

CYRANO.   do you suppose they're there?

POET. Are—

CYRANO.   they come to bring devotion,

POET. Eh?

CYRANO. Or see a talking bear?

POET. En—

CYRANO.   y monster, sirs, will do. But

POET. Oh—

CYRANO.   the real monster's you.

[*He indicates the crowd around him. Nobody applauds. There is puzzlement: why is he behaving like this? DE GUICHE comes in with CUIGY, BRISSAILLE and other gentlemen.*]

295 **CUIGY.** Monsieur de Guiche, with a message from the Marshal—

DE GUICHE. [*taking a chair.*]
　　—Who wishes to convey his necessarily impartial
　　Felicitations on your flamboyant bravery.

CROWD. Bravo!

CYRANO.   I respect his judgement.

DE GUICHE.   He
　　Was incredulous, until the testimony
300 　　Of these gentlemen convinced him.

CUIGY.   After all, we
　　Saw everything.

LE BRET. [*softly, to CYRANO.*]
　　　　　　What's the matter?

CYRANO.   Quiet, Le Bret!

LE BRET. You look as though you're suffering. What did she s—

CYRANO. No!

DE GUICHE. This incident at the Porte de Nesle
　　Is, I hear, one of many—notorious,
305 　　Glorious—I'm told it's not easy to tell.
　　You're one of these wild Gascons?

CYRANO.   That is so.

DE GUICHE.   These hairy, head-high heroes—

FIRST CADET.   One of us.

DE GUICHE.   So these are the famous, infamous—

CARBON.   Cyrano,
Present them.

CYRANO.   I obey your order.

CARBON.   Go!

310   **CYRANO.**   These are the Gascony cadets—
Captain Castel-Jaloux's their chief—
Braggers of brags, layers of bets,
They are the Gascony cadets.
Barons who scorn mere baronets,
315   Their lines are long and tempers brief—
They are the Gascony cadets,
With Castel-Jaloux as their chief.
They're lithe as cats or marmosets,
But never cherish the belief
320   They can be stroked like household pets
Or fed on what a lapdog gets.
Their hats are fopped up with aigrettes
Because the fabric's come to grief.
These are the Gascony cadets.
325   They scorn the scented handkerchief,
They dance no jigs or minuets.
They cook their enemies on brochettes,
With blood as their apéritif.
These are the Gascony cadets,
330   Compact of brain and blood and beef,
Contracting pregnancies and debts
With equal lack of black regrets.
Cuckolds, cuckoo, and cry 'Stop thief!'
Too late. Await the bassinets.
335   Castel-Jaloux there is the chief
Of these—the Gascony cadets.

DE GUICHE.   [*mildly impressed.*]
It's fashionable for a gentleman's retinue
To contain a poet or so, so how would you
Like to join mine?

CYRANO.　　　　　　　　I don't like retinues.

340 **DE GUICHE.**　　Your performance in the theatre managed to amuse
　　　My uncle, Cardinal Richelieu. You know, I could,
　　　If you cooperated, do you a little good
　　　In that direction. I suppose, like everyone,
　　　You've written a play in verse?

LE BRET.　　　　　　　　Your *Agrippina*—
345　　　Here's your chance to get the thing put on.

DE GUICHE.　　Take it to him.

CYRANO.　　[*half tempted.*]　　Hm.

DE GUICHE.　　　　　　　　He's expert in the drama
　　　Himself. Just let him, you know, reshape a scene, a
　　　Character. He'll be happy to rewrite
　　　The odd line here, the odd line there.

CYRANO.　　　　　　　　　　I might,
350　　　If I thought of anyone's changing a single comma
　　　Didn't make my blood curdle—

DE GUICHE.　　　　　　　　But when he likes a thing
　　　He pays munificently.

CYRANO.　　　　　　　The golden ring
　　　Of my own writing, lines that soar and sing
　　　Through my brain and bones and blood, is my best reward.

355 **DE GUICHE.**　　You're proud, sir—dangerously so.

CYRANO.　　Dangerous to myself? I think not, my lord.
　　　To others—well—

[*They look at each other in reciprocal dislike. A* CADET *comes running in with a drawn sword on which torn and battered hats are transfixed.*]

CADET.　　　　　　　Cyrano! Cyrano—
　　　I say—look what we found out on the street
　　　This morning—feathers from the fowl you put to
360　　　Flight.

CARBON.　　Nicely mounted, very neat,
　　　Ready for the trophy-room.

CUIGY.　　　　　　　　He'll be not too
　　　Pleased with himself today, the scoundrel who
　　　Hired the hirelings who were underneath.

BRISSAILLE.　　Does anyone know who it was?

DE GUICHE.   Why yes, I do.

365   I was—the scoundrel.

[*The noise of merriment ceases at once.*]

                                        I don't use my own teeth
         For biting insolent poets. I leave it to
         Hirelings to chew them up.

CYRANO.   Rather endentulous
         Hirelings.

CADET. [*unabashed.*]
                    Cyrano, what would you like us
         To do with these? Boil them, broil them, bake them?
370   There's plenty of grease on them.

CYRANO.   Monsieur could take
         Them and return them to his friends.

[*So saying, he grabs the sword and lets the hats cascade from it at DE GUICHE's feet. DE GUICHE stands and hides his fury.*]

DE GUICHE.   I want my chair!
         My porters! Now! As for you, monsieur—

A VOICE IN THE STREET.   The chair and porters of Monseigneur
         Le Comte de Guiche!

[*DE GUICHE's temper is under control. He speaks to CYRANO almost amiably.*]

DE GUICHE.   Monsieur, have you read *Don*
375   *Quixote*?

CYRANO.   Read it? I've practically lived it.

DE GUICHE.   Ponder on—

PORTER.   The chair is here.

DE GUICHE.   —The windmill chapter.

CYRANO.   Ninety-one.

DE GUICHE.   If you fight with windmills, they'll swing their heavy spars
         And spin you down to the mud.

CYRANO.   Or up to the stars.

[*Silence. DE GUICHE leaves. All the notables leave with him—CUIGY and BRISSAILLE somewhat abashed—and the crowd follows, not too happy now about calling CYRANO 'mon ami'. The CADETS settle at a table and are eagerly served with food and drink by RAGUENEAU. CYRANO salutes with exaggerated courtesy those who do not dare take their leave of him.*]

CYRANO.   Messieurs—messieurs—messieurs—

LE BRET.   You've done it again.

380   CYRANO.   Stop growling.

LE BRET.   No, to be quite accurate, when
    A man has achieved an unprecedented ecstasy
    Of excess, you can't say he's done it again.

CYRANO.   I did it on principle. Excess, you see,
    Is not excessive when it's been conceived
385   On principle. My success is achieved
    Only by excess.

LE BRET.   Oh, if only you'd stop
    Trying to be the three musketeers and Don
    Christ Quixote rolled up into one,
    You'd make your way, you'd wing up to the top.

390   CYRANO.   Up to the top. What would you have me do?
    Seek out a powerful protector, pursue
    A potent patron? Cling like a leeching vine
    To a tree? *Crawl* my way up? Fawn, whine
    For all that sticky candy called success?
395   No, thank you. Be a sycophant and dress
    In sickly rhymes a prayer to a moneylender?
    Play the buffoon, desperate to engender
    A smirk on a refrigerated jowl?
    No, thank you. Slake my morning mouth with foul
400   Lees and leavings, breakfast off a toad?
    Wriggle and grovel on the dirty road
    To advancement and wear the skin of my belly through?
    Get grimy calluses on my kneecaps? Do
    A daily dozen to soften up my spine?
405   No, thank you. Stroke the bristles of some swine
    With one hand, feel his silk purse with the other?
    Burn up the previous incense of my mother-
    Wit to perfume some bad bastard's beard?
    No, thank you. When all pride has disappeared,
410   Sail stagnant waters, with madrigals for oars,
    The canvas filled with the breath of ancient whores
    Or unfructified duennas? Be the pope
    Of some small literary circle and softsoap
    Editors and reviewers? Shall I look

415	For a lifetime's reputation from one book
	And then give up the agonizing art
	As far too wearing? No, thanks. Shall I start
	Finding true genius only in imbeciles
	And acneous hairy oafs? Let out shrill squeals
420	At being neglected by the columnists?
	Live in a fog of fear, grope through the mists
	Of scheming calculation? No, thanks. Is it
	Best I should think it best to make a visit
	Rather than make a poem? Relish the savour
425	Of stuffy salons? Seek condescension, favour,
	Influence, introductions? No, no, no,
	Thank you, no. No, thank you. But to go
	Free of the filthy world to sing, to be
	Blessed with a voice vibrating virility,
430	Blessed with an eye equipped for looking at
	Things as they really are, cocking my hat
	Where I please, at a word, at a deed, at a yes or no,
	Fighting or writing: this is the true life. So
	I go along any road under my moon,
435	Careless of glory, indifferent to the boon
	Or bane of fortune, without hope, without fear,
	Writing only the words down that I hear
	Here—and saying, with a sort of modesty,
	'My heart, be satisfied with what you see
440	And smell and taste in your own garden—weeds,
	As much as fruit and flowers.' If fate succeeds
	In wresting some small triumph for me—well,
	I render nothing unto Caesar, sell
	No moiety of my merit to the world.
445	I loathe the parasite liana, curled
	About the oak trunk. I myself am a tree,
	Not high perhaps, not beautiful, but free—
	My flesh deciduous, but the enduring bone
	Of spirit tough, indifferent, and alone!
450	**LE BRET.** Alone, yes, tough, yes, but indifferent—no.
	An indifferent man, God knows, doesn't go
	Around as you do, seeking enemies.
	CYRANO. And *you* make friends. With all deference, is
	That gift not rather a canine one? You grin
455	At your big pack of friends, your lips tucked in

Like a hen's arse. You love new friends. I'm glad
To make new enemies.

LE BRET.   Oh, this is—

CYRANO.   Mad?
Call it my little foible. To displease
Is my chief pleasure. I love hatred. He's
460   My best friend who admits he's my worst foe.
You've no idea how bracing it is to go
Marching upright against a volley of venom,
In the sights of bloodshot eyes of angry men, am-
Ong the spit of bile and froth of fear,
465   Cooled, as by rain, by those gentle drops. My dear
Friend, you're indifferent. Who on earth could hate your
Guts? You're soft and warm and bland good nature,
One of these Italian cowls, comfortable, loose,
Designed for softening the chin. Now, I've no use
470   For anything but an iron collar, full of spikes,
Made ever spikier by new dislikes.
It makes me hold my chin up, walk erect,
A Spanish fetter blessed with the effect
Of a French halo. Hate is not a prison.
475   Hate is the god of day, newly arisen.
Hate is a heat that disinfects my soul.
Hate is an archangelical aureole.

LE BRET.   [*nodding*]
I understand, my friend. Be bitter, proud,
Before your foes or the indifferent crowd,
480   But tell *me* that she doesn't—

CYRANO.   Not so loud.

[*He is in agony. He does not see that* CHRISTIAN *has come in. Shy, aware of the enmity of the south for the north, he sits apart from his new colleagues.*]

FIRST CADET.   Cyrano, tell us about it.

CYRANO.   Presently.

FIRST CADET.   The story of this combat ought to be
A good example for this new one here,
This new-pupped, unwiped whelp, this soft-boiled egg
485   That's trickled down from Normandy.

CHRISTIAN.   I beg
Your pardon?

[*His accent becomes a subject of mockery.*]

FIRST CADET.　Pardon. One word in your ear,
　　　　Monsieur de Neuvillette. There's a subject we're
　　　　Too discreet to mention. It would be
　　　　Like talking about rope in a house where a man
490　　Has recently hanged himself.

CHRISTIAN.　　　　　　　　　What subject?

CADET.　　　　　　　　　　　　　　See.

[*He puts his hand on his nose.* CYRANO, *talking with* LE BRET, *sees and hears nothing of this exchange.*]

CHRISTIAN.　You mean Cyrano's?

SECOND CADET.　　　　　　You violate a ban
　　　　Merely by using the word. Most dangerous.
　　　　He cleft a man asunder once because
　　　　He had a cleft palate and spoke through his—

495　　THIRD CADET.　Just mention anything cartilaginous,
　　　　And—queeeek!

FIRST CADET.　　　If you want life's chronicle to be brief,
　　　　You need do no more than take out your handkerchief.

[*They look solemnly at* CHRISTIAN. CHRISTIAN *sees that* CARBON *has joined* CYRANO *and* LE BRET. *He gets up and addresses him.*]

CHRISTIAN.　Captain!

CARBON.　　　　Monsieur?

CHRISTIAN.　　　　　　　　What ought a man to do
　　　　When Gascons boast too much?

CARBON.　　　　　　　　　　He ought to show
500　　That Normans have their share of bombast too.

CHRISTIAN.　Thank you, captain. That's all I wished to know

[*He goes to a chair and sits astride it like a horseman. The* CADETS *call* CYRANO.]

FIRST CADET.　The story!

SECOND CADET.　　　　Let's have the story!

THIRD CADET.　[*rather drunk.*]　　　　Tell us the tale
　　　　Of what really happened at the Porte de Nesle.

FOURTH CADET.　[*more drunk.*]
　　　　A triumph that could have been calamcalamcalamitous.

505   **CYRANO.**   Very well. My version.
      [*In hexameters.*]
      There, then, was the enemy. Here, then, was I,
      Marching towards them. Like a great clock in the sky
      The moon pulsed out at me. But suddenly I saw pass
      A cottonwool cloud across it, like an angel cleaning its glass,
510   And night fell equally black on myself and my lurking foes—
      So black that a man couldn't see even as far as his—

   CHRISTIAN   Nose.

[*There is astonishment.* CYRANO *quakes. He addresses his captain.*]

   CYRANO.   Who is that man there?

   CARBON.   The new man who came
      This morning.

   CYRANO.   This morning.

   CARBON.   This morning.

   CYRANO.   This morning.

   CARBON.   His name
      Is Christian de Neuvi—

   CYRANO.   [*in control.*]   Oh, I see. Where was I?

515   **CHRISTIAN.**   God knows.

   CYRANO.   [*raging.*]   Mordious!

[*The* CADETS *cannot at all understand his sudden restraint.* CYRANO *speaks naturally again.*]

                             A cloud over the sky
      So black a man couldn't see even as far as his toes.
      And I marched along, reflecting that, to save that base
      Drunken poetaster, I might be spitting in the face
      Of some great man, a prince, well able to have at me
520   Right in the—

   CHRISTIAN.   Nose.

   CYRANO.   [*controlled but sweating.*]
                      Teeth. But still, imprudently,
      I marched. Why, though, should I stick my—

   CHRISTIAN.   Nose.

CYRANO. Finger in that pie?
Was Gascon impetuosity a match for Parisian cunning?
Could I, a Gascon, ever live down the ignominious running
Of my—

CHRISTIAN. Nose?

CYRANO. [*ditheringly.*]
Legs? But I said to myself: 'On, on,
525 Son of Gascony, be brave, do what has to be done,
March, Cyrano, march.' Then out of the porridge-thick
Darkness came the first thrust, and caught me a flick—

CHRISTIAN. On the nose.

CYRANO. I parried, and found myself—

CHRISTIAN. Nose to
nose—

CYRANO. With a hundred garlicky ruffians, from whom such a stink
arose—

530 **CHRISTIAN.** That your nose took fright.

CYRANO. With my head lowered like
a bull
I charged—

CHRISTIAN. Nose to belly.

CYRANO. [*desperate.*] Belly of St Thomas Aquinas!

[*He prepares to leap upon* CHRISTIAN, *who is quite unperturbed.* CYRANO *controls himself with an effort and continues, concludes rather.*]

Then I released the full
Flood of my boiling wrath. Screams of pain rang out.
Then a sword came—sneeeeeeet—and I responded—

CHRISTIAN. [*high-pitched.*] Snout.

CYRANO. [*furiously.*]
535 Out of here, everybody out of here!

FIRST CADET. That's better.
At last the sleeping tiger wakes again.

CYRANO. Out, out—leave me alone with this man.

SECOND CADET. Rissoles on your menu, Ragueneau.

THIRD CADET. Get a
Coffin ready.

RAGUENEAU.   I feel myself turning into
540   A napkin.

CYRANO.   Come on, hurry it, everybody out!

FIRST CADET.   What's going to happen—

SECOND CADET.   Doesn't bear thinking
        about.

THIRD CADET.   The imagination—

FIRST CADET.   Positively—

SECOND CADET.   Boggles.

CYRANO.   Out, you.

[He kicks off the last CADET. CHRISTIAN, standing, waits, sword ready for drawing. CYRANO then stupefies him.]

CYRANO.   Come to my arms!

CHRISTIAN.   [stupefied.]   Monsieur?

CYRANO.   You have courage. I like
        courage.

CHRISTIAN.   I don't think I quite—

CYRANO.   I'm her brother.

545   CHRISTIAN.   Whose brother?

CYRANO.   Hers.

CHRISTIAN.   I don't think I quite—

CYRANO.   Hers, hers.
        Hers.

CHRISTIAN.   Oh, my God—her brother?

CYRANO.   Near enough.
        What they term a fraternal cousin.

CHRISTIAN.   And she's—
550   And she's—and she's—

CYRANO.   Told me everything? Yes.

CHRISTIAN.   She loves—she loves—she loves me?

CYRANO.   Perhaps.

CHRISTIAN.   Oh, I'm
        Overjoyed to make your acquaintance.

CYRANO.   This
        Is what they call a change of heart.

CHRISTIAN.   Forgive me, please,
555   Forgive me.

CYRANO.   You're a handsome devil, no
Doubt about that.

CHRISTIAN.   Oh, if you only knew how much
I admire you, sir.

CYRANO.   How about all those noses?

CHRISTIAN.   I take them back, every single nostril.

560   CYRANO.   Roxane expects a letter from you—tonight.

CHRISTIAN.   [in deep distress.]
Oh, no.

CYRANO.   What?

CHRISTIAN.   I ruin everything if I write.

CYRANO.   How?

CHRISTIAN.   Because I'm such a damned fool.

CYRANO.   The way
You tackled me was not damned foolish.

CHRISTIAN.   Oh,
I can find the words when mounting an attack—
565   Call it military wit. But I don't know
How to mount, assault—the things to say,
I mean, when it comes to a woman. I become
Paralytic, tonguetied, speechless, dumb.

CYRANO.   That's explicit enough.

CHRISTIAN.   If only I
570   Had the words—

CYRANO.   I have the words. All I lack
Is looks.

CHRISTIAN.   You know her.

CYRANO.   Know her.

CHRISTIAN.   Know that she's so
Exquisite, sensitive—one false word and I blow
Any illusion she may have skyhigh.

CYRANO.   If only I had somebody like you
575   As the interpreter, if I may put it so,
Of my dumb music.

CHRISTIAN.   If only I had your wit,
      Your eloquence—

CYRANO.   Well, why not borrow it?
      And, in return, I'll borrow your good looks.
      There's promising algebra here: you plus I
580   Equal one hero of the story books.

CHRISTIAN.   I don't think I quite—

CYRANO.   So I don't see why
      I shouldn't give you words to woo her with.

CHRISTIAN.   You—give—me—?

CYRANO.   Call it a lie,
      If you like, but a lie is a sort of myth
585   And a myth is a sort of truth. No reason why
      Roxane should be disillusioned. Let's start
      A fruitful collaboration.

CHRISTIAN.   You frighten me!

CYRANO.   What scares you is the thought of the time when she
      And you are alone, and you cool down her heart
590   With breath unwarmed by words. Well, have no fear:
      My words will be with you, glued to your
      Lips. What do you say?

CHRISTIAN.   I say what I said
      At first: I don't quite—

CYRANO.   Understand. Unsure
      About my motive? Simple: it's pure art.
595   The finest lines of the dramatist are dead
      Without the actor's partnership. One whole
      Is made from our two halves—your lips, my soul.

CHRISTIAN.   I think I see. To you it's not much better
      Than a refined amusement. Still, I'm grateful.
600   Oh God, we have to start at once—

CYRANO.   The letter.
      You mean the letter.

[*He whips it out like a conjuror.*]

                        Here it is, complete,
      Except for the address.

CHRISTIAN.   I don't quite—

CYRANO.   It
Will serve: an exercise in poetic wit.
Poets who have no mistress but their muse
605   Often do this. I could serve you up a plateful
Any time. What you must do is to use
To a solid end these airy nothings. Here—
The more eloquent for being insincere.
Provide a dovecote for these harmless doves.

[*CHRISTIAN takes the letter wonderingly and handles it as if frightened it may go off.*]

610   **CHRISTIAN.**   Will these words fit her?

CYRANO.   Like a pair of gloves.

CHRISTIAN.   But—

CYRANO.   She's a woman. It follows that she loves
Herself so well she's ready to believe
This is for her alone. It began with Eve,
That delusion of uniqueness.

CHRISTIAN.   [*sincerely grateful.*]
                                                  My dear, dear—

615   **CYRANO.**   Friend?

[*They embrace as the door opens and the* CADETS *and* RAGUENEAU *look in.* LISE *and her* MUSKETEER *appear from the living quarters.*]

FIRST CADET.   [*behind* RAGUENEAU *and* LE BRET.]
                              I daren't look. The silence here—
It's a graveyard silence.
[*Seeing.*]   What in the name—

SECOND CADET.   Of—

MUSKETEER.   [*beaming.*]   Aaaah!

LE BRET.   [*in wonder.*]
Our devil changed into a Christian brother.
Attack one nostril, and he turns the other.

MUSKETEER.   And so, at last, we can talk about—haha—
620   Lise, come here, watch this.

[*He saunters insultingly up to* CYRANO.]
                                                  Hm, what a smell—
Wine, some rare vintage. You, with that sort of carrot,
Or shall we call it an inverted parrot

Appendage, seem equipped to sniff it well.
What is it, do you think?

CYRANO.   Oh, fresh-tapped claret.

[*He strikes the* MUSKETEER *on the nose and sends him flying.* LISE *is outraged,*
RAGUENEAU *delighted. The rest cheer, patting* CYRANO *on the back as they lead
him out.* CHRISTIAN *runs after, shouting.*]

625   **CHRISTIAN.**   Her address—you didn't give me her address!

[CURTAIN.]

Act 3

Outside Roxane's house

[*The house is in a little square in the old Marais. There is a garden wall with ivy and jasmine. Over the front door of the house is a balcony that gives off a tall window open to the evening air. A tall tree shades the house. There is another house near* ROXANE's, *with a front door whose knocker is swathed to cut down noise for some reason as yet unexplained. Downstage is a stone bench. It is a glorious summer evening, but* RAGUENEAU, *who sits on the bench with Roxane's* DUENNA, *does not appreciate it. He has much to moan about.*]

RAGUENEAU. Ran away—absconded—just like that—
With that damnable musketeer—leaving me flat,
Ruined, solitary, desolate. I was ready to
Finish things off, quit this vale of—when you-know-who

5   Came along and offered me this position—
Steward to madame—

DUENNA.   But how on earth did you
Manage to get yourself into that condition?

RAGUENEAU.   Oh, Lise liked men in uniform. As for me—
Well, poets were my passion. Mars finished off

10   Everything Apollo didn't scoff.
Then Nemesis walked in, as you can see.

[*The* DUENNA *nods sympathetically, then calls shrilly.*]

DUENNA.   Madame, are you ready? We're going to be
Late.

ROXANE. [*off.*]
        I'm coming.

DUENNA. [*to* RAGUENEAU.]
                    There's this lecture on tonight
In that house there—Madame Clomire—

15   The Tender Passion.

RAGUENEAU. [*nostalgically.*]
                    Tender Passion?

DUENNA.   That's right.
      You'd better get on with your stewardizing.

[*RAGUENEAU nods sadly and gets up, walking like a broken man into the house.
ROXANE can be heard within.*]

ROXANE.   My cloak—I'm sure I left it here.

[*CYRANO can be heard approaching, singing, to an accompaniment of guitar and
treble recorder.*]

> I praise the lilies of your skin,
>   But only from afar.
20 I long to venture in
>   To where your roses are—

[*There is a discord and a cry of pain from CYRANO.*]

DUENNA.   A bit sour.

[*CYRANO appears with two musical PAGES.*]

CYRANO.   B natural, not B flat, you flat-headed naturals.

A PAGE.   You're sure, monsieur?

CYRANO.   I'm sure, monsieur. A major
25   Chord—

ROXANE.   [*on the balcony.*]
                    Is that Cyrano?

CYRANO.   Major keys
      Have major chords. Come on.
      [*Sings.*]
> And sipping as the bee mouth sips,
>   Adore them with my lips.

ROXANE.   I'm coming down.

DUENNA.   These infant prodigies—
30   Where did you find them?

CYRANO.   Won them in a wager
      On a point of Greek grammar with the Academy.
      Thank God I had them only for the day.
      [*Addressing the PAGES.*]
      You know the house of Monsieur Montfleury?
      [*They shake their heads.*]
      The fat actor?

[*They nod.*]
Go to him and play

35   A sour serenade. Tell him, if he asks, that I'm
The donor of the treat. Play piercingly.
Play dissonantly. Play for a long time.

[*The* PAGES *leave.* ROXANE *appears from her front door.* CYRANO *bows, doffs.*]

Madame, as usual, I've come to see
If our flawless friend's maintaining his sublime
40   Height of flight.

ROXANE.   Oh, my Christian—he
Is beautiful, brilliant—I love him desperately.

CYRANO. Brilliant?

ROXANE.   More brilliant even than you.

CYRANO. [*complacently.*]   I agree.

ROXANE. I've never in my life know anyone who
Could say those little things so beautifully
45   That are nothing and yet, everything. It's true
That sometimes his muse expires into a sigh—
Inexplicably—but then she revives, and he
Says, oh he says such things—

CYRANO.   Really?

ROXANE.   You
Think, as most men think, that it's impossible
50   For a man to be both bright and beautiful.

CYRANO. Talks well, does he, about love and so forth?

ROXANE.   No.
Talk is so inadequate. It's art, it's eloquence. Listen.
'The more you take my heart, the more heart have I left,
Dear heart, for loving you the more . . .'

CYRANO. [*with an author's distaste for his own work.*]
Ugh.

ROXANE.   And then: this ache
55   Of emptiness, however, bids me yearn
To seek your heart to fill it in return'

CYRANO. First too much and then too little. He'd
Rhapsodize better if he'd try to learn
To make his mind up. How much heart does he need?

60 ROXANE. Now you're teasing me. Jealousy, that's what it is.

CYRANO. Jealous? I?

ROXANE. Yes, of that talent of his.
For the last word in tenderness, listen to this:
'Ah, in your presence, such confusion grips
My heart that it grows wordless as a kiss.
65 If kisses could but wing in wingéd words,
Then you could read my letter with your lips.'

CYRANO. Not bad, not bad—a bit overwritten, though.

ROXANE. But listen to this—

CYRANO. You know them off by heart?

ROXANE. All of them.

CYRANO. [twirling his moustache.]
Very flattering.

ROXANE. He's so
70 Golden-tongued, such a master of his art.

CYRANO. Oh, I don't know—it's a sort of verbal mist,
A rhetorical fog—

ROXANE. [stamping her foot.]
A master!

CYRANO. [bowing.] If you insist.

[Meanwhile the DUENNA, who has been hovering in the garden shadows, comes running urgently towards them.]

DUENNA. Madame—Monsieur de Guiche is here. Quick, you,
Monsieur Cyrano—he may put two and two
75 Together if he sees you here—inside!

CYRANO. [going rapidly in.]
Inside, inside.

ROXANE. It's growing hard to hide
Our secret. He'll—cut me down like a tree
If he so much as guesses—

[DE GUICHE comes in. He bows low.]

Monseigneur—

[She curtsies.]

I was just leaving.

DE GUICHE. Alas, I'm leaving too.

80   For the war.

ROXANE. Alas.

DE GUICHE. This very evening. We've
    Orders to besiege Arras.

ROXANE. Arras?

DE GUICHE. Arras. Tell me, does my leaving leave
    You as cold as it seems to do?

ROXANE. Oh, no.

DE GUICHE. I find that this present prospect of leaving you
85   Leaves me quite desolate. Oh, did you know
    I'd been promoted colonel?

ROXANE. Oh, Bravo.

DE GUICHE. Yes, colonel of the Guards.

ROXANE. [*uneasily.*] The Guards?

DE GUICHE. The Guards—
    The regiment of that man who's big in words
    And the other thing—beastly de Bergerac.
90   I may, with luck, get some of my own back—

ROXANE. Ordered to Arras?

DE GUICHE. Under my command.

ROXANE. Oh, no.

DE GUICHE. What is it?

ROXANE. The flower in one's hand
    Is so suddenly depetalled. This wind, the war
    Disperses all its perfume. One loves—and then—

DE GUICHE. [*eagerly.*]
95   You've never—never spoken like this before.
    You say these things—now—for the first time—when
    I have to leave you—

ROXANE. And you said, just then,
    Something about revenge—my cousin—

DE GUICHE. Ah, yes.
    Are you for him?

ROXANE. [*with conviction.*]
                    Very much against.

100   DE GUICHE.   You see him much?

ROXANE.   As little as I can.

DE GUICHE.   I see him too much. Lately he's commenced
        Keeping company with this new man—
        Neuve or Neuville or something—

ROXANE.   Tall?

DE GUICHE.   Tallish.

ROXANE.   Fair?

DE GUICHE.   Fairish.

ROXANE.   Handsome?

DE GUICHE.   A fool.

105   ROXANE.   I've seen him, I think, but don't know him at all.
        To return to my cousin. Tell me what you
        Propose for Cyrano. Send him into the thick
        Of the fighting? He'll love that. I know what *I'd* do.

DE GUICHE.   What?

ROXANE.   Leave him here, with his precious cadets,
110   Kicking his heels. That ought to make him sick,
        While the rest of the regiment goes off and gets
        Medals and wounds and things. I know him. If you
        Want to strike at him—strike at his self-esteem.

DE GUICHE.   Oh, woman, woman—only a woman could
115   Dream up a scheme like that.

ROXANE.   The cadets will chew
        Their nails, but Cyrano will eat out his heart.
        And you'll have your revenge.

DE GUICHE.   [*coming closer.*]   You love me, then—
        A little? When you make my enemies
        Your enemies—I'd like to see that as a sign
120   Of love—

ROXANE.   [*backing away.*]
                    It could be—the sign of a start—

[*DE GUICHE takes documents from a satchel. He is, for the moment, businesslike.*]

DE GUICHE. These are the orders for the companies,
Signed, sealed, not yet delivered. This
Is for the Guards. I'll keep it. Cyrano,
So much for you, you battle-truffling swine.
125 And so you too, Roxane, you like to play
Your little games?

ROXANE. [*watching him with some apprehension.*]
Sometimes.

DE GUICHE. Sometimes I say
To myself that you and I are two of a kind.
But always I'm mad about you. Now—to find
Love trembling within you—when I have to go—
130 Intolerable. Listen. Half a mile or so
From here, in the rue d'Orléans, the order of
Capuchins has its centre of brotherly love,
Under Father Athanasius. Accordingly to
Their rule, no layman may enter. But who
135 Can bar the nephew of Richelieu? Their sleeves
Are wide enough to hide me. The regiment leaves
For the siege tonight, but without me. One
More day will make no difference. Later on
Tonight I'll come to you—masked.

ROXANE. I apologize
140 For mentioning the word—but—honour. Eyes,
Spies will be watching. If anyone should
Find out—

DE GUICHE. Pooh!

ROXANE. The war, your duty, the good
Of your family name—

DE GUICHE. A lot of nonsense. I've
A more urgent duty, a greater good—to contrive
145 The voluntary surrender of—Say yes.
Say it now.

ROXANE. No.

DE GUICHE. Say it. Whisper it.

ROXANE. My
Duty is to make you do yours. But—

DE GUICHE. Bless
You for that *but.*

ROXANE.   Oh no, you must go. Go. I
  Must make myself make you go. I must order you
150 To be my hero.

DE GUICHE.   So you *can* love—can
  Truly love—

ROXANE.   When I tremble for the safety of a man,
  I may talk of love—

DE GUICHE.   And yet you say I must go?

ROXANE. Yes, in the name of love, my dear dear friend.

DE GUICHE. I go then. This adieu means not an end
155 But a beginning. Later, then. Later, Roxane.

[*He kisses his hand effusively at her, bows, leaves. The* DUENNA *comes on, making a mock reverence.*]

DUENNA. My dear dear friend.

ROXANE.   Say nothing about
  What I did just then. If Cyrano finds out
  I stole his war from him—

DUENNA.   Yes, yes.

ROXANE. [*calling.*]   Cyrano!
  [*To her* DUENNA.]
  I must keep up appearances. We must still go
160 To this discourse on the Tender Passion.

DUENNA.   All right,
  But you've your own Tender Passion to attend to.

ROXANE.   I know.
  But Alcondre and Lysimon are speaking tonight.

DUENNA. And you're not going to listen.

CYRANO. [*coming out.*]   Listen, do.
  Monkey-chatter can be instructive.

DUENNA. [*going towards the other house.*] See—
165 They've muffled the knocker, so that we
  Shan't give the Tender Passion a heart attack.

ROXANE. [*to* CYRANO.]
  When Christian comes to see me, tell him to wait.

CYRANO. Wait? But don't you make him dissertate
  On a subject picked in advance?

DUENNA.   Monsieur Bergerac,
170   We're going in. Come on, madame, we're late.

ROXANE.   A subject?

CYRANO.   Subject.

ROXANE.   But you'll be quiet?

CYRANO.   Dumb
         As a wall, that's me.

ROXANE.   Nothing—no, everything.
         Whatever singing fantasies shall come
         Unbidden to his brain—on the subject of,
175   Naturally, love.

CYRANO.   Naturally. Love.

ROXANE.   I'll tell him to overwhelm me with excess,
         To rhapsodize, be brilliant.

CYRANO.   Good.

ROXANE.   [*fingers to lips.*]   But—shhhh.

CYRANO.   [*fingers to lips.*]
         Shhhh, as you say.

ROXANE.   Not a word.

CYRANO.   Thanks very muchhhh.

ROXANE.   Totally unprepared.

CYRANO.   Heavens, yes.

BOTH.   [*fingers to lips.*]   Shhhh.

[*The* DUENNA *having knocked, the door having been opened, the two ladies go in.*
CYRANO *goes to the edge of the garden and calls.*]

180   **CYRANO.**   Christian!

[CHRISTIAN *appears, very fashionably dressed now.*]

                        Come and have the lines thrown to you.
         I have your theme. All that you have to do,
         You lucky, lucky, lucky, is to get
         Your memory ready. This is your best chance yet
         To cover yourself in genius. So let's go
185   Round to your lodgings. We don't have much time.
         Come on, now, try to look intelligent.

CHRISTIAN.   [*forcefully.*]   No!

CYRANO.   No harm in trying to look intelli—Oh,
You mean . . . ?

CHRISTIAN.   That's right, my friend, I mean that I'm
Going to stay here, going to wait for her.

190   CYRANO.   But this is mad, this is the most head-reeling
Vertiginous lunacy. Come on, come now, sir,
Come and learn your lines.

CHRISTIAN.   No, I'm feeling
Rebellious tonight. I'm tired, yes tired
Of borrowing your lines, your letters, saying
195   What you tell me to say, dithering with stage-fright.
Oh, it was fine at first, it was like playing
A sort of game. But now, at last, tonight,
I'm past all fear. Tonight I feel inspired
With my own inspiration. I no longer doubt
200   That she loves my. My own words crash out.

CYRANO.   Limp out, trickle out. Come on.

CHRISTIAN.   No. I'm not
Entirely an analphabetic sot,
As you'll see. Thanks to you, I've learned a lot.

CYRANO.   [sardonically.]
As I see.

CHRISTIAN.   And, though I can't yet make
205   The verbal summits, I know enough to take,
By God, a woman in my arms.

CYRANO.   Bravo.

[ROXANE and her DUENNA come out of the neighbouring house, along with
exquisites of both sexes. CYRANO nods with grim satisfaction and starts to go.
But CHRISTIAN loses his confidence.]

CHRISTIAN.   [frightened.]
It's her—it's she—don't leave me, Cyrano!

CYRANO.   You're on your own, monsieur. Good luck. Goodnight.

[And so he marches off. CHRISTIAN trembles.]

ROXANE.   [to her friends.]
Good night, Barthénoide, Grémione,
210   Alcandre, Urimédonte—

DUENNA.   [insincerely.]   I was quite
Looking forward to that lecture.

[*ROXANE sees* CHRISTIAN *and calls him. The* DUENNA *nods indulgently and goes into the house. The exquisites and précieuses leave the stage. The lovers are alone.*]

ROXANE.   Christian!
Christian, you came. No matter that I missed
That discourse by an amorous theorist
Or theoretical amorist. Now the best
215 Of all of them is here. The air is sweet.
Evening is come. We are alone. That seat
Beckons. Talk. I'll listen. Shall we sit?

[*They seat themselves on that downstage bench. There is a silence, expectant on* ROXANE's *part, wretched on* CHRISTIAN's. *At length he breaks it.*]

CHRISTIAN.   I love you.

ROXANE.   So. Your theme. Embroider it,
Weave gorgeous tapestries.

CHRISTIAN.   Love you.

ROXANE.   Rhapsodies.

220 **CHRISTIAN.**   I love you so much.

ROXANE.   So much. Good. And
Then?

CHRISTIAN.   And then—I would—I would be glad if you
Loved me too. Say that you love me too.

ROXANE.   [*pouting.*]
You offer skimmed milk when I ask for cream.
Tell me *how* you love me.

CHRISTIAN.   Very much.

ROXANE.   Turn your theme
225 Into a loving labyrinth. Devote
Your discourse to the true Platonic note.

CHRISTIAN.   [*growling.*]
Oh God—I want to kiss you—kiss your throat.

ROXANE.   Really!

CHRISTIAN.   I love you.

ROXANE.   That again?

CHRISTIAN.   Oh no,
I do not love you.

ROXANE.   Good.

CHRISTIAN.   I adore you.

ROXANE.   Oh,
230   This is too much.

[*She gets up.* CHRISTIAN *too has to rise.*]

CHRISTIAN.   Forgive me, Roxane, I'm so
In love I'm growing stupid.

ROXANE.   I agree,
And that displeases me as much as though
You were growing ugly.

CHRISTIAN.   Listen—

ROXANE.   Retrieve
Your scattered eloquence. Otherwise—leave.

235   CHRISTIAN.   But I—

ROXANE.   I know. You love me. Goodnight.

CHRISTIAN.   Stay!
Wait—listen—what I have to say
Is—

ROXANE.
That you adore me. Good. Now go away.

[*She enters the house in a great huff.* CHRISTIAN *is desperate.* CYRANO *comes on.*]

CYRANO.   A great success. Felicitations.

CHRISTIAN.   For God's sake
Help me.

CYRANO.   Ah no.

CHRISTIAN.   I shall die, here and now,
240   If here and now I find no way to make
Her love me again.

CYRANO.   Heavens, you idiot, how
Do you expect me, here and now, to—

[*A light goes on in Roxane's upper window.* CHRISTIAN *is the first to see it.*]

CHRISTIAN.   Wait—
Look—see—

CYRANO. [*touched.*]
           Her window.

CHRISTIAN. [*stentorianly.*]   I shall die.

CYRANO.   Not so much noise.

CHRISTIAN.   [*whispering.*]   Die.

CYRANO.   [*looking up.*]   Hm—a cloudy sky.

245   CHRISTIAN.   Yes? Yes? Will you—?

CYRANO.   To reinstate
      You may not be easy. Still, we have to try.
      Stand there, in front of the balcony, while I
      Stand underneath and whisper the right words.

CHRISTIAN.   [*dubiously.*]
      But—

[*The* PAGES *return.* CYRANO *addresses them.*]

CYRANO.   Welcome back, my unmelodious birds.
250   You've serenaded Montfleury? Good. Now,
      You go to the corner of the street
      And you go *there*. Wait for approaching feet.
      If anyone comes by, play something—

[*They start off. He hales them back.*]

                                    Wait.
      A sad tune for a man—don't demonstrate—
255   And for a lady something shrill and sweet.
      All right, all right, be off with you.

[*The* PAGES *leave, severally.*]

CHRISTIAN.   Now how
      Do we start?

CYRANO.   Call her.

CHRISTIAN.   Roxane!

CYRANO.   A pebble or two.

[*He throws some pebbles at the window, then he gets under the balcony, while* CHRISTIAN *stands in front of it.* ROXANE *appears.*]

ROXANE.   Was somebody calling?

CHRISTIAN.   Me. I.

ROXANE.   Who?

CHRISTIAN.   Christian.

ROXANE.   [*disdainfully.*]   So.

CHRISTIAN.   I *have* to talk to you.

260 **ROXANE.** You've nothing to say to me.

CHRISTIAN. Oh, please—*please*—

ROXANE. It's clear that you love me no longer.

CHRISTIAN. [*to whom* CYRANO *whispers the right words.*]
Such heresies . . .
Such unjust slanders . . . Oh, you divinities . . .
Whose name is justice . . . witness that I love
More than mere words . . . can bear the burden of . . .

265 **ROXANE.** Better.

CHRISTIAN. Love . . . that I had thought . . . a quiet child
Discloses moods . . . so intemperate . . . and wild . . .
He crushes my . . . cradling heart.

ROXANE. Hm. Better still.
But is it not best to break that unruly will
And strangle such a monster?

CHRISTIAN. Heavens, I've tried
270 To commit that . . . venial infanticide,
But . . . the tough atomy . . . I thought to seize . . .
And crush . . . turned out an infant Hercules.

ROXANE. Good. Very good.

CHRISTIAN. His first act was . . . to ride
And rend . . . two hissing serpents . . . Doubt and Pride.

275 **ROXANE.** Quite excellent. But, since you mention doubt,
Why do your words come so—haltingly out?
It's as if your fancy suffered from, well—

CYRANO. [*in approximation to* CHRISTIAN's *voice.*]
Gout?

[ROXANE *tinkles a laugh.*]

Quick, this is getting difficult.

ROXANE. Tonight
You hesitate so strangely. Why?

CYRANO. A good
280 Question, and my answer is: each word
Gropes through the darkness, looking for your light.

ROXANE. If that were really so, my own words would
Limp, just like yours. Come, try a less absurd
Explanation.

CYRANO.   Very well. Taste this:

285 My heart is open wide—your words can't miss
So large a target. Or, heavy with the honey of
Desire, it zigzags to the orifice
Of your tiny ear, and buzzes bluderingly,
Seeking its way in, its wings a haze of love.
290 Or, should these not suffice, then, finally,
Since your words fall, they yield to gravity:
Mine have to rise and fight it.

ROXANE.   It seems to me
They fight less hard now than they had to do
A moment ago.

CYRANO.   Ah, but a moment or two
295 Of loosening up in the gymnasium
Works wonders.

ROXANE.   Am I so far above you still?

CYRANO.   So far, I fear, that one hard word could kill,
Crushing my heart like a stone.

ROXANE.   Oh, then I'll come
Down to you.

CYRANO.   No!

ROXANE.   But I want to see you. Stand
300 On that bench there—

CYRANO.   No!

ROXANE.   Such a vehement *no.*
What *is* the matter?

CYRANO.   To hold in my hand
Such exquisite joy—I dare not let go
This precious chance to speak to you—unseen.

ROXANE.   Unseen?

CYRANO.   A disembodied spirit, clean
305 Of the clogs of accident and decay. You see
A cloak of trailing blackness; you to me
Are a white gown of summer. I am a shadow
And you the quintessence of light. How can you know
What it means to roam this transitory meadow
310 Sunlit through the darkness? If ever—oh,
If ever I was eloquent—

ROXANE. You were—
Very eloquent.

CYRANO. But you have never heard till now
My true heart speaking.

ROXANE. Why not?

CYRANO. There
Was a certain obliquity, a sort of haze
315   Caused by this vertigo, this drunkenness
That afflicts all those who tremble in your presence.
But this one night it seems that I address
Your heart for the first time.

ROXANE. The first time, yes.
Your very voice is changed.

CYRANO. My heart's true essence
320   Is emboldened by this darkness to speak out.
It is myself that speaks. Where was I? Oh, forgive
This confusion, which is to me a heap
Of rose petals, a fantasy of sleep
So new, and so delicious.

ROXANE. New?

CYRANO. To live
325   A moment breathing your sustaining air,
Freed from the choking asthma of the fear
That you might laugh at me—

ROXANE. Laugh at you? Why?

CYRANO. Because of the unworthiness of a fool,
An insufficiency that seeks to clothe
330   Itself in a sunset of words. How often I
Come to pluck Hesperus out of the sky
And end by plucking flowers because I loathe
A presumption that might spark your ridicule.

ROXANE. There's good in flowers, there's sweetness.

CYRANO. Yes, yes,
335   But not enough sweetness in all of the flowers of the earth
For us, tonight.

ROXANE. You have never spoken like this,
Never before.

CYRANO. Shatter them all, these tokens—

Valentine hearts, arrows, the tinselled quiver,
Stale words, stale honey sipped in finicking drops
340 From tarnished gilded cups. What are they worth
Compared to the wild urge that shouts, that beckons
Our bodies to plunge and drown in the wild river?

ROXANE.   But the soul, the spirit—?

CYRANO.   You mean the petty rhymes
Wrung from what petty spirits call the soul.
345 I have made enough of those for you at times
When I did not dare to bare myself, as now,
To the overwhelming torrent of the night
With its panic perfumes. Oh, my God, must we
Insult nature by burbling nugacities
350 When those gold nuggets, myriad on myriad,
Enflame the heavens? Our little alchemy,
Distilling civilized exquisitries—
Might it not, in its crass self-regard,
Volatilize true feelings to the wind,
355 And, dripping wordlets, miss the one true word?

ROXANE.   Oh, but—poetry. You can't say that
Of poetry—

CYRANO.   Poetry—rhyme—a game of words.
Ah, love's too stark a force to tolerate
Such tinklings, such tinkerings. A moment comes—
360 And God help those for whom it never comes—
When love of such nobility possesses
This shaking frame that even the sweetest word,
The ultimate honey, stings like vinegar—

ROXANE.   If so,
What, when the moment comes for both of us,
365 What words will you say?

CYRANO.   In that most precious
Instant, I shall take all words that ever were,
Or weren't, or could, or couldn't be, and in
Mad armfuls, not bouquets, I'll smother you in them.
Oh God, how I love you, I choke with love, I
370 Stumble in madness, tread a fiery region
Where reason is consumed, I love you beyond
The limits that love sets himself, I love,
I love. Your name, Roxane, swings like a brazen

Bell, telling itself—Roxane, Roxane—
375   In my heart's belfry, and I tremble—
Roxane, Roxane—with each bronze, gold,
Silver reverberation. Listen, I swing
Down the rope to earth's level, to each small thing
—Trivial, forgettable, unforgettable by me—
380   That ever you do or did. A year ago,
The twelfth of May it was, at noon's striking,
You left your house with your hair dressed a different way,
The former way not being to your liking,
And you know how, when you've been looking at the sun,
385   You see red suns everywhere, embossed
On everything, so that solar flood of your hair
Blinded me and bequeathed an after-image
Of heavenly goldness touching everything
With a royal touch.

ROXANE.   [*shaken.*]   Yes—this is—love.

390   CYRANO.   Love, the parasitic heavenly host,
A terribly jealous god has seized me with most
Wretched fury—and yet he seeks not to possess,
He is only mad to give. So my happiness
Is there to augment yours—even though
395   You forget, or never knew, the scourge of its flow.
I ask no more than to listen, twice, or thrice,
To the laughter born out of the sacrifice
Of mine. Each glance of your eyes begets some new
Virtue in me, new courage. Oh, can you
400   See this, feel it, understand? Do you sense
My heart rising towards you in this intense
Stillness, whose perfumed velvet wraps us close?
This night I speak, you listen. Never in my most
Reckless unreasonable dream have I hoped for this.
405   Now I can gladly die, knowing it is
My words that make you tremble in the blue
Shadow of the tree. For it is true—
You do tremble, like a leaf among the leaves,
Yes, and the passion of that trembling weaves
410   A spider filament that seeks me now,
Feeling its way along the jasmine bough.

ROXANE.   Yes, I do tremble, and I weep, and I
Am yours. I love, you have made me—

CYRANO.   Ah, to die,
      Death is all I need now after this
415   Summit gained. I ask one thing—

CHRISTIAN.   [bluntly breaking the spell.]
                                           A kiss.

ROXANE.   What?

CYRANO.   [quietly seething.]
                      Ooooooh.

ROXANE.   You asked for something.

CYRANO.   Yes—
      Too quick, too soon.

CHRISTIAN.   [quietly but urgently.]
                            Well, you got her into this
      State. Why shouldn't I get some benefit?

CYRANO.   Yes, it's true. I did ask. But I was too
420   Impetuous. I was—hurled into it.

ROXANE.   You ask no more than that?

CYRANO.   No more?

CHRISTIAN.   [eagerly.]   No. Yes.

CYRANO.   No more is no more than a void, a nothingness.
      I asked too much, I ask you now to rebuff
      My importunity.

CHRISTIAN [quietly shaking him.]
                      Why, why?

CYRANO.   Enough.
425   Be quiet, Christian.

ROXANE.   What are you saying?

CYRANO.   Myself
      Was being angry with myself for going
      Too far. I said: 'Be quiet, Christian.'
      That was rude, I suppose. Somebody's coming—

[We hear from the distant PAGES a bright tune and a sad accompaniment.]

      By the sound of it, a woman and a man.

[And old CAPUCHIN enters. He carries a lantern and is evidently looking for a
particular address. CYRANO addresses him.]

430   Ah, I see what they mean—a priest. Diogenes?
        Back from the dead, looking for honesty?

    CAPUCHIN.   No, sir. The name is—er—Madame Robin.

    CHRISTIAN.   Here's a damned nuisance.

    CYRANO.   You seem to be
        On the wrong track. Go straight.

[*He points. The* CAPUCHIN *nods his thanks.*]

    CAPUCHIN.   Thank you, my friend.
435   I'll pray for you.

    CYRANO.   May grace and fortune attend
        Your holy cucullus.

    CAPUCHIN.   [*pausing, suspicious.*]
                     Eh?

    CYRANO.   Cucullus.

[*The* CAPUCHIN *realizes, having forgotten the term, that* CYRANO *means his hood. Satisfied, he moves on and off.*]

    CAPUCHIN.   Yes, yes, I see.

    CHRISTIAN.   Get that kiss for me.

    CYRANO.   No.

    CHRISTIAN.   That kiss for me.

    CYRANO.   No.

    CHRISTIAN.   Sooner or later I—

    CYRANO.   Sooner or later, true,
        It has to be, that labial conjunction,
440   A historical necessity, since she
        Is beautiful and, all unworthy, you
        Glow in the perfume of the unearned unction
        Made up of youth and strength and comeliness.
        But I must be the agent of her *yes*.

[CHRISTIAN *grinds his teeth*, ROXANE, *who went in on the appearance of the* CAPUCHIN, *is out again on the balcony.*]

445   ROXANE.   Has he gone? Are you there?

    CYRANO.   Yes.

    ROXANE.   We were speaking of—
        Of a—

CYRANO.   Kiss. The word is sweet enough,
　　　　And yet your lips are shy of saying it.
　　　　If the word burns them, what is your presage of
　　　　The thing itself? Fear should consume you. Yet
450　　After all you've glided insensibly
　　　　From mockery to a smile, from a smile to a sigh,
　　　　From a sigh to a tear. Now slide from a tear to a kiss.
　　　　It's but a heartbeat's distance from that to this.

ROXANE.   [*as ready, or almost, as* CHRISTIAN.]
　　　　Oh, do be quiet.

CYRANO.   [*comfortably settled for a lecture.*]
　　　　　　　　　Soon. In a moment. How
455　　Shall we define a kiss? The sacrament of a vow,
　　　　The lightly stamped seal of a promise, the endorsement of
　　　　A promissory note on the bank of love,
　　　　The very O of love in the expectant lips,
　　　　Eternity in the instant the bee sips,
460　　The music of the spheres on the lark's wing,
　　　　A flower-tasting eucharist, a ring
　　　　Forged of two rings, red alchemized to gold.

ROXANE.   Enough.

[CHRISTIAN *nods vigorously.*]

CYRANO.   [*taking his time.*]
　　　　　　　　　So noble a thing, that, so we're told,
　　　　The Queen of France could not, from her fabulous hoard,
465　　Find a richer jewel to bestow on an English lord.

ROXANE.   [*impatiently.*]
　　　　Indeed?

CYRANO.   Indeed. And, like Lord Buckingham, I
　　　　Too have had my mournful silences, my
　　　　Unspeakable adoration of majesty—in you.
　　　　Like him, I am sad and faithful.

ROXANE.　　　　　　　　　　Like him too
470　　You are beautiful.

CYRANO.　　　　　So I am. I'd forgotten.

ROXANE.　　　　　　　　　　Come.

CYRANO.   [*to* CHRISTIAN.]
　　　　You heard what she said.

ROXANE.   Taste your flower.

[CHRISTIAN, *as before, is hesitant when it comes to the act.*]

CYRANO.   Get up there.

ROXANE.   Let us savour our
   Souls conjoined in our lips.

CYRANO.   Now what
   In hell's name are you waiting for?

CHRISTIAN.   I'm not
475   Sure, really, this is the right time—

ROXANE.   Here's
   Your instant infinity, your music of the spheres.

CYRANO.   Mount, you animal!

[*He pushes* CHRISTIAN *to the tree, whose branches he climbs with ease to reach the balcony.* CHRISTIAN *takes* ROXANE *in his arms. They kiss.*]

CHRISTIAN.   Ah—Roxane!

CYRANO.   [*not looking.*]   It appears
   He's at his banquet—the banquet I prepared,
   Only to end as its Lazarus. Still, I'm spared
480   One crumb, I suppose, one wishbone. And this is
   The knowledge that it's my words that she kisses
   And not his lips. So—let's be cheerful, then.

[*The double music starts up once more from the* PAGES.]

   Woman? Man? It's that Capuchin again.

[*He lightly runs into the shadows and then reappears, running, as if just arriving.*]

   Ho there!

[ROXANE *and* CHRISTIAN *disengage.*]

ROXANE.   Who is it?

CYRANO.   Cyrano. Is Christian
485   Up there by any chance?

CHRISTIAN.   [*with a show of surprise.*]
                 Cyrano!

CYRANO.   That Capuchin
   Is here again. It's something for you, Roxane.
   You'd best come down.

[ROXANE *and* CHRISTIAN *go in. The* CAPUCHIN *appears.*]

CAPUCHIN.   Madame Robin lives here.
I have it on very good authority.

CYRANO.   Rolin?

CAPUCHIN.   Robin.

CYRANO.   I thought you said Rolin.

CAPUCHIN.   Robin.
[*Bleating like a sheep.*]
490   Robiiiiiiiin.

CYRANO.   I hear. It wasn't very clear
Before. One letter can make a difference. Not L—B.

CAPUCHIN.   [*suspiciously.*]
How did you know I have a letter? Oh, I see.
I see.

[*ROXANE and CHRISTIAN come out of the door.*]

ROXANE.   Letter?

CAPUCHIN.   For Madame Robin.

ROXANE.   I am she.

CAPUCHIN.   A very noble lord gave it to me
495   To give to you.

ROXANE.   De Guiche!

CHRISTIAN.   He dares?

ROXANE.   He won't
Dare any more—not now.

[*They look at each other ardently and can hardly restrain themselves from embracing.*]

CAPUCHIN.   Some holy matter, I don't
Doubt.

[*ROXANE, having torn open the letter, reads it to CHRISTIAN while CYRANO tries to interest the CAPUCHIN in horticulture.*]

ROXANE.   'The drums are beating. The regiment
Is ready for the march. I have already sent
The story about that I have gone on ahead,
500   But in fact I'm here in the convent—as I said
I would be. I'm sending this by an old
Sheep-headed monk who, naturally, has not been told
Its content. I must see you tonight. I must.

Your smile both beckons and maddens. I hope and trust
505　You have already forgiven my audacity
And will give a welcome to him who hopefully
Sincerely etcetera etcetera.'
[*She addresses the* CAPUCHIN.]
　　　　　　　　　　　　　Father! This letter
Concerns you.

CAPUCHIN.　　　Does it? Does it?

ROXANE.　　　　　　　　　　So I'd better
Read it to you.

CAPUCHIN.　　　Very well, very well.

510　ROXANE.　It's terrible.

CAPUCHIN.　　　　　　Come, my child.

ROXANE.　　　　　　　　　　'Mademoiselle,
It seems His Eminence the Cardinal
Will have his way, whatever you say or do.
That is why I send this note to you
By a very holy, intelligent, discreet
515　Capuchin. Instruct him, please, to meet
These my instructions, which are that he is
At once, in your house, to perform the ceremonies
Of holy matrimony—' Oh, this is tyrannical.

CAPUCHIN.　　Courage, daughter.

ROXANE.　　　　　　　　　'His Grace the Cardinal
520　Demands the nuptials of you and Christian.
This is hard news, I know. But all that you can
Do is resign yourself to the command
Of His Eminence, who sends his blessing and
His wishes for much happiness. I end
525　With my own good wishes. Your humble friend,
Etcetera etcetera.'

CAPUCHIN.　　　　I knew it, I knew
He was truly noble, one who could not do
A thing that was not wholly holy. Who
Is the bridegroom?

[*He looks at the two men.* ROXANE *breaks down, or pretends to.*]

ROXANE.　　　　　　Oh, this is awful.

CAPUCHIN.　[*to* CYRANO.]　　　　You?

530   This will of God, daughter, is often obscure.

CHRISTIAN.   It's me—I am the bridegroom.

CAPUCHIN.   Are you sure?

ROXANE.   [*quickly.*]
        'Postscript. Give to the convent, in my name,
        One hundred and twenty louis. Signed: the same.'

CAPUCHIN.   A worthy lord. It's very rare to fine
535   Blue blood allied to such a generous mind.
        Daughter, resign yourself.

ROXANE.   I *am* resigned.
        [*To* CYRANO.]
        De Guiche will come. For God's sake hold him there.
        He mustn't enter before—

CYRANO.   [*to the* CAPUCHIN.]   How long will it take?

CAPUCHIN.   Oh, fifteen minutes, sir.

CYRANO.   You'd better make
540   It five. In. In. I need fresh air.

[*The* CAPUCHIN *goes in with the soon-to-be-happy couple.*]

        I also need to distract his lordship. Where?
        How? Up here. I think I have my plan.

[*He gets up into the branches of the tree. Gloomy music sounds.*]

        Ah, by the sound of it, a man,
        Very much a man in a minor key.
545   Come, then. Not too high. Protect me, tree.

[*DE GUICHE fumbles his way on, masked.*]

        A matter of a voice? Will he know it's me?
        Let me open the door to my origins. Cric crac.

[*He winds himself up like a toy. He speaks like a Gascon, not a Parisian. He puts his hat back to front and puts his cloak over it.*]

        Cyrano—be true de Bergerac.

DE GUICHE.   Did that blasted Capuchin deliver? Damn this mask—
550   I can't see—

[*CYRANO leaps down gracefully.* DE GUICHE *starts.*]

                    Where did you fall from, may I ask?

CYRANO.   The moon.

DE GUICHE.   The moon?

CYRANO.   What time is it?

DE GUICHE.   Is he mad?

CYRANO.   What time—country—day of the month—of the year?

DE GUICHE.   Let me—

[He tries to get to Roxane's front door. CYRANO stays in the way.]

CYRANO.   I'm dizzy, dazed, befuddled—

DE GUICHE.   Monsieur—

CYRANO.   I fell. I've fallen. You wish to know where from?

555   DE GUICHE.   The moon, you said.

CYRANO.   The moon. Dropped like a bomb,
        And I don't mean that metaphorically.

DE GUICHE.   [trying to get past him.]
        Please—

CYRANO.   A second—maybe a century—
        I lost all sense of time during my fall.
        I was in this kind of saffron-coloured ball—

560   DE GUICHE.   Good. Let me pass.

CYRANO.   Where? Where? Don't trifle with
        This shattered sensorium. What is this place
        On which I've tumbled like an aerolith?

DE GUICHE.   An aerolith?
        Allow me—

CYRANO.   I had no choice, hurtling through space,
        Oh my point of arrival. *Where am I?* Ah, that face—
565   Black—are you an oppressed colonial?

DE GUICHE.   This is a mask.

CYRANO.   Venice! A carnival!

DE GUICHE.   [still trying to pass.]
        A lady is waiting for me.

CYRANO.   Ah, now I know—
        Paris. Where else could it be? Paris. So
        This is where the ethereal typhoon
570   Has dumped me. What a voyage. Dust of the moon,
        Asteroid fragments cling like sleep to my eyes,

Planet-fur on my spurs, blond comet-hairs
On my coat—

DE GUICHE.   Allow me—

CYRANO.   Can you see the Great Bear's
Toothmark in my calf? This bump on my thigh's
575   From the hurled waterpot of Aquarius.
You've no idea of the zodiacal fuss
I initiated. I fell into one of the dishes
Of Libra's scales, and look—scales from the Fishes
—Hard to scrape off. Grab my nose with your fingers,
580   Give it a squeeze and it will spurt out pure
Milk—

DE GUICHE. *Please.*

CYRANO.   From the Milky Way. I broke a string as
I glissaded over the Lyre. Ah, you can be sure
There's a book in this, a perilous record of risks.
I shall use these stars on my cloak as asterisks.

585   **DE GUICHE.** Good. Now if you'll excuse me—

CYRANO.   Do forgive.
You're impatient to be apprised of the creatures that live
In the lunar caverns, and to know the morphology
Of its cucurbitous rotundity—

DE GUICHE. What I want now—

CYRANO.   Is to know how I got up
590   There—My special invention, yes?

DE GUICHE.   Mad.

CYRANO.   First, I swear
It has nothing to do with Regiomontanus's
Eagle or Archytas's pigeon—ornithology
Doesn't come into it—stupid birds, anyway.

DE GUICHE. Mad, but he's been to a university.

595   **CYRANO.** No! My mode of spatial travel is
Painfully original. Mode—did I say?
Modes. I've invented six techniques whereby
To violate that blue virginity
Up there.

[*DE GUICHE grows interested in spite of himself.*]

DE GUICHE.   Six?

CYRANO.   Six. Let me specify.
600   I strip myself as nude as a candle, place
       Around that nudity a carapace
       Covered with crystal vials of morning dew.
       The sun sucks up the dew, and sucks me too.

DE GUICHE.   So. That's *one*.

CYRANO.   Another one. I escape
605   From earth in a ship of icosahedral shape—
       Struck with ten burning mirrors. They rarefy
       The air. The rare air lifts me, and I fly.

DE GUICHE.   Two.

CYRANO.   Or I mount a machine forged in the figure
       Of a grasshopper, activated by a trigger
610   That sets off successive charges of saltpetre.
       I jerk off into space. What could be neater?
       Sweeter?

DE GUICHE.   Three.

CYRANO.   Smoke always tends to soar.
       I fill a globe with smoke and—

DE GUICHE.   That makes four.

CYRANO.   This next may seem fantastic. Bright Apollo,
615   Who rules the sun, he likes to suck and swallow
       The marrow of the oxen of the sun.
       I smear myself with that—and, swish, it's done.

DE GUICHE.   Five.

CYRANO.   Finally, monsieur, I sit or stand
       Upon an iron plate. And in my hand
620   I clutch a magnet. This I throw—and—throw—
       The iron lurches after, as you know.
       I can do that indefinitely.

DE GUICHE.   Six.
       Which did you choose of these ingenious tricks
       To make your recent voyage into heaven?
625   Not that I believe you.

CYRANO.   Number seven.

DE GUICHE.   And what's the seventh way?

CYRANO.   You're going to see.

[CYRANO *makes strange noises and gestures.*]

     DE GUICHE.   What?

     CYRANO.   Can't you guess what's happening to me?

     DE GUICHE.   No.

     CYRANO.   It's nearly time, sir, for high tide.
     The moon is calling.

[*And, indeed, the moon, long occluded, has at last emerged from behind the clouds.*]

                       I must stand beside

630   The ocean, having wallowed in it first.
     My hair is dripping wet. The lunar thirst
     Pulls at it, then the rest of me. I soar
     Free as an angel, as I did before,
     Tumbling to earth a quarter of an hour ago.

635   The time, my lord, is up. And so—

     DE GUICHE.   And so?

[CYRANO *resumes his normal voice, adjusts his cloak and hat. His nose shines in the moonlight.*]

     CYRANO.   A marriage has been celebrated.

     DE GUICHE.   What?
     Am I drunk or something? That voice. It's not—
     That nose—It is.

     CYRANO.   [*with a courtly reverence.*]
               At your service. Cyrano.

[*The wedding procession appears,* RAGUENEAU *and Roxane's* DUENNA *holding candles, the* DUENNA *crying, the two* PAGES—*who must have entered the house by the back door—playing festive music.* ROXANE *and* CHRISTIAN *beam.*]

     DE GUICHE.   You! He! Clever, mademoiselle.

640   **ROXANE.**   Baroness.

     DE GUICHE.   [*to* CYRANO.]
               You, monsieur, you did that well.
     You could have charmed a saint poised on the sill
     Of heaven. You ought to write that book.

     CYRANO.   I will.

     CAPUCHIN.   My lord, the knot is tied you bade me tie.

DE GUICHE.   As I can see. You, *baroness*, bid goodbye
645   To your paint-fresh husband.

ROXANE.   Bid good—Why?

DE GUICHE.   [*to* CHRISTIAN.]
     Your regiment leaves tonight, sir. Be so good
     As to report at once.

ROXANE.   You mean—for the war?

DE GUICHE.   That is what regiments usually leave for,
     Milady.

ROXANE.   But you—surely—I understood
650   The cadets were not going.

DE GUICHE.   They are and always were.
     [*To* CHRISTIAN.]
     Here is the order. Pray deliver it, sir.

ROXANE.   [*falling into her husband's arms.*]
     Oh, Christian!

DE GUICHE.   [*sneering, to* CYRANO.]
                    The wedding night is still a good
     Way off.

CYRANO.   That thought disturbs me less than it should.

CHRISTIAN.   Your lips again—

CYRANO.   Come on. Enough. Let's go.

655   **CHRISTIAN.**   Oh, you don't know how hard it is.

CYRANO.   I know.

[*Drums can be heard in the distance, also the shrilling of a trumpet.*]

DE GUICHE.   We're marching.

[*He salutes sardonically and marches off.*]

ROXANE.   [*in great distress.*]   Take care of him, Cyrano.
     Keep him out of danger.

CYRANO.   [*hanging on to* CHRISTIAN.]
                    All right, I'll try,
     But I can't really promise.

ROXANE.   Be sure he keeps warm and dry.

CYRANO.   As far as is soldierly possible.

ROXANE.   Keep him away

660   From other women.

CYRANO.   Not even the odd little chat?

ROXANE.   No! And make him write me every day.

CYRANO.   [*at attention, emphatically.*]
Madame, I can certainly promise you that.

[*They go. The women weep.* RAGUENEAU *and the* PAGES *wave. Drums and trumpets.*]

[CURTAIN.]

Act 4

The Siege of Arras

[*We are at the post occupied by Captain Carbon de Castel-Jaloux's company. In the background there is a rampart; beyond it a plain stretches away to the horizon, with earthworks covering it. In the distance are the walls of Arras and the silhouette of its roofs against the sky. There are tents, weapons, drums, a campfire. SENTRIES stand at spaced-out intervals. Some of the CADETS sleep round the fire, under blankets. It is a cold dawn. LE BRET and CARBON keep watch: they are pale and emaciated. CHRISTIAN, asleep, is even more so; he is also restless. There is as yet no sign of CYRANO.*]

> **LE BRET.**   Shocking.
>
> **CARBON.**   Very.
>
> **LE BRET.**   Intolerable.
>
> **CARBON.**   Intolerably so.
>
> **LE BRET.**   [*loudly*]
> God curse it!
>
> **CARBON.**   If *you* want to curse, keep it low.
> You'll wake them.

[*Some of the sleepers stir.*]

> Shhhh. Sleep, sleep.
> Who sleeps, dines.
>
> **LE BRET.**   Who takes a nap takes a snack.
> 5   But if, like me, you're an insomniac
> You don't get much in the way of dinners, you know.

[*There is firing offstage. LE BRET is angry.*]

> God damn that blasted insomniac musketry.
> It'll wake our babies.

[*Men raise their heads from their blankets.*]

Sleep, deep, deep.
It isn't reveille yet.

[*There is more firing.*]

CARBON. Just the usual crack
10   At Cyrano coming back home.

[*The raised heads are lowered.*]

A SENTRY. [*offstage.*] Halt, who goes there?

CYRANO. [*offstage.*]
Cyrano de Bergerac.

ANOTHER SENTRY. [*on the parapet.*]
Halt, who—

CYRANO. [*appearing.*] Bergerac,
Imbecile.

LE BRET. Thank God, as usual, you're back.

CYRANO. [*descending, motioning him not to waken the sleepers.*]
Shhhhh.

CARBON. Not wounded yet?

CYRANO. No, they've got
Into the habit of missing me.

LE BRET. Risking your life
15   Before breakfast to post a letter—mad. Not,
Of course, that there *is* any breakfast.

CYRANO. What
Must be done must be done. I promised his wife,
As I must call her, that he'd speak to her by post
If he couldn't speak on the pillow. Pale as a ghost,
20   Poor devil, starving to death.

CARBON. We all are.

CYRANO. I know,
But he seems to show it more than most.
If only that poor child could see him—Still handsome, though.

LE BRET. You'd better get some sleep.

CYRANO. Don't growl at me,
You old mother-bear, and don't worry either. I'm
25   Pretty careful crossing the Spanish lines.

I just wait till they're drunk.

CARBON. You might
Consider bringing something back sometime
For us.

LE BRET. *Jamòn. Huevos. Vino.*

CYRANO. I would if I
Didn't, as you know, have to travel light.
30 Today, though, there appear to be signs
That the French are going to dine or else to die.

CARBON. What signs?

CYRANO. I'm not sure. But you'll see.

LE BRET. What a mess.
We're besieging Arras, and yet it's we
Who are doing the starving.

CARBON. Besieging Arras, yes.
35 And all the while His Eminent Gorgeousness
The Cardinal Prince of Spain is besieging *us*.

CYRANO. Perhaps somebody will get down to besieging *him*.

LE BRET. Not funny. Our chances don't get any better,
And yet you grin instead of looking grim.
40 Risking your life every day to send a letter.
You're unnatural. What sort of a father and mother—
Never mind. Where are you going?

CYRANO. To write another.

[*He goes into a tent. Drums signal the dawn. We hear the distant voices of officers waking their men.*]

CARBON. Damned drums. Another nutritious sleep
Gone to the devil. Poor devils. I know
45 What their first words are going to be.

[*The* CADETS *wake, groaning.*]

FIRST CADET. God, I'm so
Hungry.

CARBON. [*prodding the sleepers.*]
Come on, out of it.

SECOND CADET. Oh, no.

THIRD CADET. Not one step.

FOURTH CADET.   [*looking in a polished cuirasse.*]
                                    Yellow as saffron cake,
    My tongue.

FOURTH CADET.   [*waking with a start.*]
                            Cake—who said cake?

FIRST CADET.   Very indigestible air,
    This time of day.

CARBON.   Come on.

SECOND CADET.   I'm not going to make
50   Another move.

THIRD CADET.   I'd give my coronet
    For a mousetrap. And I wouldn't care
    Whether it was cheese or mouse that I found there.

SIXTH CADET.   [*looking out of his tent.*]
    I tell you this: if my stomach doesn't get
    Something to stop its roaring, it's going to stay,
55   Like Achilles, in its tent all day.

LE BRET.   [*at* CYRANO'S *tent-flap.*]
    Cyrano—come out.

FOURTH CADET.   Bread before bullets.
    I'm perfectly prepared to forgo the butter.

LE BRET.   [*more urgently.*]
    Cyrano—come on. There's a mutinous mutter
    Ready to brew. Take their minds off their gullets.
60   Tell them a tale or something—

THIRD CADET.   [*rushing up to* FIRST CADET.]
                                    What's that you're chewing?

FIRST CADET.   Gun wad fried in the choicest axle grease.
    Good rich country, this. Would you care for a piece?

[*Two* CADETS *enter, one with a gun, the other with a fishing rod.*]

SEVENTH CADET.   Home from the hunt.

EIGHTH CADET.   Fishing in the river Scarpe.

[*Two other* CADETS *rush to them. They yell severally.*]

CADETS.   What have you got there? Fish? Game? Pheasant? Carp?

65   **EIGHTH CADET.**   A gudgeon.

    SEVENTH CADET.   A sparrow.

    CADETS.   Mutiny!

    LE BRET.   [*with great urgency.*]   Cyrano!

[CYRANO *comes tranquilly from his tent, a pen in one hand, a book in the other, a helmet on his head.*]

    CYRANO.   This noise is very distracting.

[*There is a guilty silence.* CYRANO *addresses* FIRST CADET.]

                         You. I see
You've something on your mind.

    FIRST CADET.   My stomach.

    CYRANO.   We
All suffer the same vacuity.

    SECOND CADET.   But you seem to enjoy it.

    CYRANO.   Good for the figure.

70   **THIRD CADET.**   Something to eat, for God's sake.

    CYRANO.   There are bigger
Things than food. Still—one salad bowl.

[*He takes off his helmet and places it on the ground. The* CADETS *look into it as though, by magical conjuration, food will appear in it.*]

    SECOND CADET.   I don't see any salad.

    CYRANO.   Feed your soul
With Homer's *Iliad*.

[*He throws in the book. The* CADETS *growl.*]

    FIRST CADET.   Oh God, when I
Think of all those swine guzzling away
75   Back in Paris at their six meals a day,
Like his Holy Grace and Cardinal—grrrr—

    CYRANO.   [*reasonably.*]   But
Why envy His Grace his grease? Better to die
Of inanition than a loaded gut.
The gate of heaven is narrow, and the thin
80   Man has the easier chance of sidling in.

    FIRST CADET.   [*angrily.*]
Don't try to feed us with epigrams. Fine words
Butter no parsnips.

SECOND CADET.   [*deliriously.*]
                    Parsnips—in a white sauce.

THIRD CADET.   I don't care much for parsnips. Oh, good
        Lord, what am I saying?

CYRANO.   *I* am saying this:
85   I'd rather die on pointed elegances—
        Fine words, as you call them—under a sky
        Of saffron sunset than wail and weep and cry
        About my rumbling innards. Rather die
        Saying a good thing for a good cause
90   Than dream of licking goose-grease from my paws,
        Die at the hands of a worthy enemy
        Rather than be degraded by the eclipse
        Of death in a soft bed. I want to depart
        This life with honourable steel piercing my heart
95   And a piercing epigram upon my lips.

SECOND CADET.   But we're hungry.

CYRANO.   The whole world's hungry. You
        Think only of yourselves.

[*We now notice that the old* FLUTEPLAYER *of the company has come in starving but
stoical. He sits at the back of the stage.* CYRANO *addresses him.*]
                        Here, Bertrandou—
        Old shepherd as you were, play on your pipe
        To these poor little lambs who grouse and gripe
100   At the griping of their guts. Put pipe to mouth
        And pipe some of the old airs of the south,
        Whose every note smiles like a little sister,
        In which we hear, through a nostalgic mist, a
        Smoke of memory, the voices of friends—
105   A melody whose lazy line ascends
        Like the thin woodsmoke of the cottages
        Of our homeland—a pungent tune that is
        The very distillation of our speech.
        Your flute, that gnarled old warrior, let him reach
110   Back, while your fingers touch the stops and dance
        A minuet of sparrows, beyond the chance
        That chose him, shaped him, notched him, changed him to
        A little glory of ebony. Let him, through you,
        Recall his days as a reed of the river, before
115   He lost his innocence and went to war.

[BERTRANDOU *plays a melancholy folk tune.*]

Listen, you Gascons, now you hear no more
The shrilling martial fife. It's a woodland cry,
Not a banshee of the battle shrieking high
But the cool cantilene the goatherds finger.
120   Listen—it's the hill where the night mists linger,
The valley, and the good earth like red meat,
The plains like a storm of emeralds, the sweet
Greenness of spring nights on the Dordogne.
Listen, you Gascons—it is all Gascogne.

[*They listen quietly to the flute tune. The odd tear is furtively wiped.*]

125   **CARBON.**   You're making them cry.

CYRANO. Yes—out of homesickness,
A nobler hunger than that of the flesh.
They're feeling a starvation in their hearts,
Not in their viscera.

CARBON. Still, it hurts
Their manhood.

CYRANO. Weakens them? Not so. I'll flush
130   The heroic scarlet to their arteries
Back in an instant. All that's needed is—

[*He makes a signal. The drums start beating. The* CADETS *start up, rush for their arms, run to the parapet.*]

CADETS.   What—where—what is it—where is it?

CYRANO.   [*to* CARBON.] See?

[*But the* CADETS *think that* CYRANO *was warning them of the approach of their colonel. He is coming.*]

SECOND CADET.   Ach—Monsieur de Guiche is on his way.

THIRD CADET.   He makes me—

FOURTH CADET. Not so much as he makes me.

[*They return to their former positions, depressed.*]

135   **FOURTH CADET.**   Sick, eh? You're not the only ones.
What with the lace collar on his corselet—

THIRD CADET.   Always the little courier—

FOURTH CADET. Very much
The nephew of the cardinal.

CYRANO.　[*always fair.*]　　　Nevertheless,
　　Gentlemen, he's one of Gascony's sons.

140　THIRD CADET.　A counterfeit. The real Gascons, us,
　　Are a bit mad, but he's a bit too sane.
　　Rational. A rational Gascon's dangerous.

LE BRET.　He's pale. At least he shows that common touch.

FOURTH CADET.　Oh, nobody doubts that he can feel the pain
145　Of hunger, just like us poor bastards, but
　　Those jewels on his belt make the cramps in his gut
　　Sort of glitter, like the sun on ice.

CYRANO.　Do you want him to see you suffering? Get out your dice,
　　Your cards. Smoke your pipes. Come on there, try and look
150　As if you liked this famine. I'll read this book—
　　Descartes.

[*The* CADETS *obey.* CYRANO, *who has taken the volume from his pocket, starts to
read. Silence.* DE GUICHE *comes in, elegant but haggard.*]

DE GUICHE.　Good morning.

[*There is a silence.*]

　　Black looks as usual, eh? Right, gentlemen—
　　The mountain-hovel nobility, the beefless barons
155　*A la sauce béarnaise,* the Périgord princelings are
　　Above respecting their colonel. Very well, then.
　　Knowing the squalor of your rabbit warrens,
　　I know how little your code of conduct matters.
　　Call me a crawling courtier, a politician,
160　Resent my steel covered with Genoese lace.
　　I spurn your standards. To be a proper patrician
　　You have to be a pauper. It's a foul disgrace
　　To be a Gascon and not go in tatters.
　　This dumb insolence asks for punishment. I've a mind
165　To leave that task to your captain. You, sir, find
　　Something fitting in the *Manual
　　of Military Law.*

CARBON.　　　　I'm afraid that's impossible.
　　I pay my men from my own pocket. And I obey
　　Battle orders only.

DE GUICHE.　　　　Indeed? Well, you and they
170　Will soon have your chance of obedience. I see
　　Your prospective resentment. Jealousy!

Your conduct under fire, apparently,
Doesn't compare with mine in any way.
How many of you, squatting on your haunches,
175   Could do the thing that I did yesterday?
I lashed the Count de Bucquoi out of Bapaume,
Pouring my men on his in avalanches.
I charged three times.

CYRANO.   [*without looking up from his book.*]
                          But you failed to bring home
Your white scarf.

DE GUICHE.   [*pleased.*]   So it's already got around,
180   That story, has it?

CYRANO.   Tell us.

DE GUICHE.   When
The third charge beckoned and I was rallying my men,
To my astonishment I suddenly found
I was being thrust with a throng of fugitives
Into the enemy's lines. The Spaniard gives
185   No quarter—I was in danger of being shot.
So what did I do? Thought quickly. Got
Shot of the white scarf that marks my rank
And thus—anonymous, inconspicuous, blank—
Escaped and rallied my own force. Ah yes,
190   It worked. From the brink of death to a crash
Of victory. What do you think, my friend,
Of that little display of resourcefulness?

CYRANO.   This. A man's white plume is his panache,
His visible soul, not a thing to lend or spend.
195   It's the shining badge of his scorn of his enemies.
Henry of Navarre, Henry the Fourth of France,
Outnumbered in the enemy's advance,
Never even dreamed of jettisoning his.

[*Quiet satisfaction is registered among the* CADETS.]

DE GUICHE.   But the point is: my device was a success.

200   CYRANO.   True. But an officier never resigns easily
His privilege of being a target for the enemy.
Your courage and mine differ in this, monsieur—
If I'd been present at that heroic affair,
When you dropped your scarf I'd have picked it up then and there

205   And worn it myself.

> **DE GUICHE.**   Always boasting.

> **CYRANO.**   No.
> Lend it to me tonight and I'll lead the charge
> With your white scarf over my shoulder.

> **DE GUICHE.**   Ah, these large
> And vacuous gasconnades. You're safe, as you know,
> With that offer. Our intelligence understands

210 That that sector still lies in the enemy's hands,
> And my scarf lies on the river bank. The river
> Is swept by their artillery. No one could ever
> Reach that scarf alive.

[CYRANO *slowly draws the scarf from his pocket. He hands it to* DE GUICHE *without moving from his place. Indeed, he turns a page of his Descartes. The quiet satisfaction of the* CADETS *is manifested in jubilant pipe-puffs.* DE GUICHE *shows no emotion. He takes the scarf.*]

> **CYRANO.**   With my compliments.

> **DE GUICHE.**   Thank you. This bit of white will do very well

215 To make a signal—a signal, that, to tell
> The truth, I was hesitant about making.
> But now, gentlemen, no more hesitance.

[He *gets up on to the parapet and waves the scarf vigorously.*]

> **SENTRY.**   Look—there's a man there running away.

> **DE GUICHE.**   And taking
> My signal with him. My pet Spanish spy.

[*The* CADETS *no longer affect indifference.* CYRANO *is alert.*]

220 **CYRANO.**   Spy?

> **DE GUICHE.**   Yes. He tells his masters what I
> Pay him to tell them.

> **CYRANO.**   [*with disgust.*]   A traitor.

> **DE GUICHE.**   I suppose so,
> But a very useful traitor. Now, what was it we
> Were talking about? Ah yes. You may as well know
> Our marshal's plan. You might find it interesting.

225 Last night we saw an opportunity
> With reasonable luck, of revictualling
> The army. In silence, covered by a good black

Night, the marshal marched to Doulens, where
Our supplies are. There's a very fair chance that he
230   Will reach them. But to be sure of getting back
In safety, he's taken an exceptionally
Large force with him. A good half of our army
Is absent from the camp.

CYRANO.   Thank God the enemy
Don't know that.

DE GUICHE.   [*smiling*]   Oh, but they do, they do.
235   They're going to attack us.

CYRANO.   Ah.

CARBON.   Ah.

DE GUICHE.   My spy,
A very reliable and pliable spy who
Tells me everything, asked me where I would
Prefer the Spanish attack to be made. My reply
Was that he should go out and wait between
240   The lines and watch for my signal. That point should
Be the point of the Spanish advance.

CARBON.   You mean—?

DE GUICHE.   [*expansively.*]
I mean, gentlemen, that this is all for you.

CARBON.   Very well, let's get ready.

DE GUICHE.   Another hour.

FIRST CADET.   [*sardonically.*]   Oh, good.

DE GUICHE.   As you will doubtless all have understood,
245   The aim is to gain time. We're not sure when
The marshal will return.

CARBON.   And to gain this time?

DE GUICHE.   [*blandly.*]
Gentlemen, you will all be so very good
As to lay down your lives.

CYRANO.   [*with equal blandness.*]
                      Would it be reasonable
To call this—well, revenge?

DE GUICHE.   I won't pretend

250   That I care the least damn about any of you.
     But since you all consider you're no end
     Of fine brave warriors and—this is hard to do,
     Admittedly—leaving out the personal,
     You're the obvious choice. If you want that to mean
255   I serve my king by serving my own spleen,
     I will not contradict you.

CYRANO. [*pleasantly.*]   Well, that's candid.
     May we offer our thanks?

DE GUICHE. [*sneering.*]   You, sir, whose bliss
     Is to engage a hundred singlehanded,
     Ought to be rather looking forward to this.

[CYRANO *turns his back on him and addresses the* CADETS.]

260   **CYRANO.**   There are, as you know, six chevrons on the old
     Arms of Gascony, six—blue and gold.
     There's going to be a seventh. You don't need me
     To tell you what the colour has to be.

[*All this time* CHRISTIAN *has been seated quietly, unmoved, unhearing, arms resignedly crossed.* CYRANO *goes over to him.*]

     Christian—

CHRISTIAN.   [*quietly.*]
     Roxane.

CYRANO.   I know.

265 **CHRISTIAN.**   I should like to say goodbye to her, to put
     My whole heart—

CYRANO.   In a letter. I thought of that.

CHRISTIAN.   Let me see it.

CYRANO.   You really want to?

CHRISTIAN.   Why not?
     I'm supposed to have written it.

[CYRANO *somewhat reluctantly takes a package from his breast and hands it to* CHRISTIAN. CHRISTIAN *looks curiously at something on it.*]

         What?

CYRANO. Yes?

CHRISTIAN.   This spot—this little circle—to me
270   It looks very much like a tear.

CYRANO.   [*embarrassed.*]   Oh, well, you know
   How it is. When a poet writes a poem, he
   Is frequently moved by his own fiction. I admit
   I've written a moving letter. I tried
   Not to be moved, but I *was* moved. Just a bit.

CHRISTIAN.   [*wonderingly.*]
275   You mean to say—you *cried?*

CYRANO.   [*stoutly.*]   Yes. I cried.
   And why not? Dropping a tear or two—this is
   In the best heroic tradition. Ajax cried, Ulysses,
   Hector. To die, I suppose, is little enough,
   Even to die in the hot morning of youth.
280   But never again to see the one we love,
   That's horrible—And the horrible bare truth
   Is that I never—we never—you—

[CHRISTIAN *looks very curiously at him.* CYRANO *is saved from further
embarrassment by a noise of trundling wheels, off, the cry of the* SENTRY.]

SENTRY.   Look at that!

CARBON.   [*rushing up to the parapet.*]
   What is it?

SENTRY.   [*incredulous.*]
          A coach and horses!

[*The* CADETS *rush up to see.*]

CADETS.   What?
   Here in the camp? It's coming from the enemy lines.
285   Fire on it! No, the coachman's making signs.
   He's shouting something. On His Majesty's
   Service. Impossible. No. Can't you hear it? His
   Majesty's Service—

DE GUICHE.   [*amazed.*]   What, the King?

CARBON.   Fall in!

DE GUICHE.   Hats off, in line, come on, you ragged lot.
290   A royal reception.

CARBON.   Drums at the ready! Begin!

[*The* CADETS *are lined up, the drums roll. Uncovered, all stand like ramrods.
Onto the stage comes a coach, with driver and tigers.*]

DE GUICHE.   Lower the step. Open the door.

[LE BRET *obeys. The door opens and discloses* ROXANE, *fresh, smart, smiling.*]

ROXANE.   Good morning.

DE GUICHE.   [*gaping.*]
  You—the King's service.

ROXANE.   The one and only king—
  Love.

CYRANO.   [*overcome with the madness of it.*]
    Oh God in heaven.

CHRISTIAN.   [*tottering.*]   You—here—but why?

ROXANE.   This siege of yours has lasted too long.

CYRANO.   I
295   Daren't look at her.

DE GUICHE.   You can't stay here.

ROXANE.   Why not?
  Give me a drum to sit on.

[*One is brought. She sits, gay, beautiful, breathing Parisian chic.*]

                          Thank you. What
    A journey it's been. A patrol very rudely shot
    At my coach. It looks, doesn't it, as though
    It's been magicked out of a pumpkin—you know—
300   Cinderella—Good morning again. Why so sad,
    All of you? Do you know, it's quite a way
    From Arras. Cyrano, I'm terribly glad
    To see you.

CYRANO.   Roxane. You'd better tell us how—

ROXANE.   I found your army? I can't tell it now
305   Too long a story. But what horrors. Grey
    And murky battlefields, corpses and casualties—
    If *that's* your king's service, mine's better than his.

CYRANO.   But this is madness. How did you get through?

ROXANE.   Easy, really. All we had to do
310   Was trot along. If some hidalgo or don
    Thrust in his head to know what was going on,
    I put on my best smile. And—please, I don't mean
    To disparage the French—but, really, I've never seen
    Such courtesy, such gallantry. Bowing low,
315   Or throwing a salute, they let us go.

CARBON.   Didn't they ask you where you were going?

ROXANE.   Often.
And when I told them—well, the news would soften
Their ferocity even more. All I had to say
When we were challenged was 'I'm on my way
320   To see my lover.' They couldn't have been sweeter.
They bowed and murmured: '*Vaya, señorita.*'

CHRISTIAN.   But Roxane—

ROXANE.   I know. 'Husband' is what I *should*
Have said, of course. But that would have done no good.

CHRISTIAN.   You don't seem to—

ROXANE.   What's the matter?

DE GUICHE.   Madame, you
325   Cannot stay here.

CYRANO.   You must go away.

LE BRET.   Quickly too.

CHRISTIAN.   You must.

DE GUICHE.   At once.

ROXANE. [*pouting.*]   Christian, do
You want me to go?

CYRANO.   There's the small matter of
A battle.

ROXANE.   Have your battle. I stay with my love,
My husband. If he dies, we die together.

330   **DE GUICHE.**   This sector of the line—it's doubtful whether
Anyone can survive—

CYRANO. [*grimly.*]   And that is why
He put *us* here.

ROXANE.   I see. You want me to be
A widow?

DE GUICHE.   I swear I had no such—

ROXANE.   I swear I
Am staying here. Call it temporary
335   Madness. Besides, it's a—new experience.

CYRANO.   So
The future chronicles of France can show

A *précieuse* could be heroic?

ROXANE. [*hurt.*]   Cyrano,
Remember I'm your cousin.

FIRST CADET.   We'll defend you.

ROXANE.   Thank you. I never doubted that, my friend.

SECOND CADET.   You
340   Can smell perfume all over the camp.

[*He totters. It may be because of hunger.*]

ROXANE.   [*preening herself in a mirror.*] I bought
This hat specially for the battle. Isn't it time,
Monsieur le Comte, you got it ready?

DE GUICHE.   I'm
Going to inspect my cannon. I'd never have thought
It possible—There's time to change your—

ROXANE.   I stay.

345   DE GUICHE.   I'm going.

[*Shaking his head at this female obstinacy, he does so.*]

FIRST CADET.   She stays.

CADETS.   [*severally.*]   Lend me your comb. Please may
I borrow that brush? This tunic's a disgrace.

ROXANE.   [*to CARBON.*]
No! Nothing is going to make me budge from this place,
His place.

CARBON.   [*having sighed deeply.*]
Very well. Let me present
My friends and comrades—gentlemen whose intent
350   Is to die bravely—here—before your face.
Baron de Peyrescous de Colignac—

FIRST CADET.   Madame.

CARBON.   Baron de Casterac de Cahuzac. Vidame
De Magouyre Estressac Lébas d'Escarabiot.
Chevalier d'Antignac-Juzet. Baron Hollot
355   De Blaganc-Saléchan de Castel-Crabioules.

ROXANE.   So many names!

FIRST CADET.   They're all we have.

CARBON.   If you'll

Be good enough to open your hand—

[*ROXANE does so and lets fall her handkerchief.* CARBON *picks it up.*]

ROXANE.   But why?

CARBON.   We lost the company flag. This will fly high
  Shedding perfume over the camp in its place.

360 **ROXANE.**   It's very small.

CARBON.   Yes, but it's genuine lace.

[*The handkerchief is affixed to a pike and set on the parapet during the following.*]

FIRST CADET.   I could die happy now, if only I'd
  Even a walnut climbing down inside.

CARBON.   Ignoble—to talk of food in the presence of
  So exquisite a lady.

ROXANE.   But I'd love
365 Some breakfast—a little pâté, a cold bird,
  Wine. Would you be good enough—? Absurd,
  You think? It's all there in my coach.

FIRST CADET.   What?

SECOND CADET.   *What?*

ROXANE.   Partridges, pheasants, *crème brûlée*—the lot.
  But it has to be carved and served, the sauce reheated
370 If you wish. Look at that man there, seated
  On the coachman's box. You recognize him? A very
  Precious man.

[*The coachman pulls off his hat and muffler and reveals himself. The* CADETS *hail him with joy.*]

CADETS.   Ragueneau!

ROXANE.   Poor boys.

CYRANO.   [*kissing her hand.*]   Our good fairy.

RAGUENEAU.   Gentlemen—

CADETS.   Bravo!

RAGUENEAU.   The Spaniards let it through—
  The wine, the poultry, and the pastry too.

[*He unloads the coach, with the assistance of the two tigers and the* CADETS. CYRANO *has something more urgent than food to attend to. He tries to get* CHRISTIAN *to himself, with no success.*]

375   CYRANO.   Christian—

RAGUENEAU.   Distracted by their gallantry,
    They missed the galantine.

CYRANO.   A word with you.

RAGUENEAU.   These cushions here are stuffed with pigeons—see!
    Preoccupied with Venus's face and grace,
    They missed these trophies of Diana's chase.

CYRANO.   [urgently.]
380   We have to talk—

ROXANE.   Spread the board. Christian,
    Make yourself useful.

[To a sprightly tune from BERTRANDOU's flute and the spanking of a drum, the victuals are spread downstage. The CADETS leap on to the cold fowls and gorge. ROXANE supervises.]

SIXTH CADET.   Well, at least we scoff
    Before the blasted bullets see us off.
    Give me a drumstick for this blasted drum.

[Meaning a chicken leg for his hollow stomach. He sees ROXANE come near and changes his coarse language for something more courtly.]

    Delicious—a celestial viaticum.

RAGUENEAU.   [bringing out wine.]
385   Flagons of rubies, jars of potable gold.

ROXANE.   [to CHRISTIAN.]
    Quick, where's the cutlery?

RAGUENEAU.   These lanterns hold
    More precious stuff than light.

[He detaches the coach lamps and starts pouring from them into glasses held by the cadets.]

CYRANO.   [grabbing CHRISTIAN.]   We have to talk.

RAGUENEAU.   The handle of my whip—is all pure pork.

[He strips off its integument and discloses a long sausage. This is seized, broken, munched.]

ROXANE.   Even if the rest of the army has to starve,
390   At least the Gascons have a joint to carve—
    Before—we're—carved.

[There is an instant's cessation of eating at her words. But it is soon resumed.]

And if de Guiche arrives—

FIRST CADET. Nothing for him.

ROXANE. Come, now, forks, spoons, knives,
Plates.
[*To a gorging* CADET.] Plenty of time. Drink this.

[*She gives him a full glass.*]

You should

Chew, not gulp. You're *crying?*

FIRST CADET. [*sobbing and eating*] It's too good.

ROXANE. [*an energetic hostess*]
395   Come—white or red? Bread for Monsieur Le Bret.
A little pastry? Toast and duck pâté?
Vin de Bourgogne. Chicken. Try a wing.
Christian?

CHRISTIAN. [*serving out.*]
Thank you. I couldn't eat a thing.
Why did you come?

LE BRET. [*eating, but also keeping watch.*]
De Guiche!

ROXANE. I'll tell you soon.

400   **CYRANO.** Stow everything. Knives, forks, plates, that spoon—

[*Meaning one that a* CADET, *busy with a whole fowl, has tucked behind his ear.*]

Bones, crumbs, the lot. Ragueneau, get up there.
Everything hidden? Fine.

[*The stowing of the victuals is done with astonishing speed.* DE GUICHE *enters, sniffing.*]

DE GUICHE. Something smells good.
You—you've changed colour.

FIRST CADET. It's this bracing air.

DE GUICHE. And *you* look cheerful.

SECOND CADET. So a soldier should
405   When the enemy's on his way.

DE GUICHE. Captain, you too
Look unnaturally healthy.

CARBON. Oh?

DE GUICHE.   [*to* ROXANE.]
And as for you,
Have you changed your mind?

ROXANE.   [*emphatically.*]   No.

DE GUICHE.   [*forcefully.*]   Go while you can.

ROXANE.   No.

DE GUICHE.   [*sighing.*]
Very well, then. Give me a musket. I
Am staying too.

CYRANO.   Spoken, sir, like a man.
410   At last you're showing Gascon fortitude.

DE GUICHE.   I don't desert ladies in danger.

FIRST CADET.   Why
Don't we give him something?

[*Something formerly held in suspension in his mouth he now openly chews.*]

DE GUICHE.   You mean food?

SIXTH CADET.   [*somewhat drunk.*]
Food in all its multiple manifestations.

DE GUICHE.   [*with great scorn.*]
Do you think I'd eat your leavings?

CYRANO.   Congratulations.
415   You're making progress.

DE GUICHE.   I fight, sir, and I fast.
This condemned man requires no breakfast, not—
Pocapdedious—like this motherless brood.

CYRANO.   Hear that—*Pocapdedious*? It seems we've got
A new recruit. He's one of us at last.

[*The* CADETS *cheer, some of them ironically.* CARBON *comes up.*]

420   **CARBON.**   My pikemen are lined up—accoutred, armed.

DE GUICHE.   [*to* ROXANE.]
Madame, will you inspect them with me?

ROXANE.   Charmed.

[*He offers his arm, which she takes. They go off together.* CYRANO *leads* CHRISTIAN *downstage.*]

CHRISTIAN.   Something to say, you say?

CYRANO. Important.

CHRISTIAN. You'd better
Speak quickly.

PIKEMEN. [off.] Vivat! Vivat!

CYRANO. Listen—

CHRISTIAN. What?

CYRANO. Roxane is going to speak not of a letter—
425 But of letters.

CHRISTIAN. Well?

CYRANO. Not just a few. A lot
The time has come to open what was hid.
You wrote a great deal more than you thought you did.

CHRISTIAN. *What?*

CYRANO. Look at it this way, I had the task
Of articulating for you. I didn't ask
430 Whether I should write or not. I wrote
Without mentioning it. When I assume a commission I devote
A sort of silent attention—

CHRISTIAN. But in God's name, how?
We're under siege, we're cut off totally.

CYRANO. Well—before dawn—it's easy enough, you see.
435 I'm able to cross the lines.

CHRISTIAN. [on whom a great truth is beginning to dawn.]
So. I see it now.
I've written more than I thought. To be precise,
How many times? Once a week, say? Twice?
Three time? Four?

CYRANO. Rather more.

CHRISTIAN. Every day?

CYRANO. [with some shame.]
Yes. Every day. Twice.

CHRISTIAN. I see. They say
440 There's only one thing that will make a man
Mad enough to—

[ROXANE is coming, alone, from the parapet.]

CYRANO. Quiet. She is coming.

[*CHRISTIAN greets her in great perturbation of mind.* CYRANO *leaves.*]

CHRISTIAN.   Roxane.

ROXANE.   And now at last, dear Christian—

CHRISTIAN.   Now at last
  You can tell me why you risked—

ROXANE.   At last I can.
  Blame your letters, if I can speak of blame.
445 That lyric flood from the battlefield. Not a day has passed
  Without their burning up my day—a flame
  That blinded me at last to danger—

CHRISTIAN.   So,
  Just for a bundle of love letters—

ROXANE.   Oh no!
  You don't know your own genius. Oh, it's true
450 There once was an evening of jasmine, lilac, rose,
  When I began to adore you. Your soul arose
  In perfume to my window, the true you
  Made itself known in a voice, but then that voice
  Sang to me everyday. I had no choice
455 But to come running. If patient Penelope
  Had received such letters from her lord Ulysses,
  She would not have woven woven endlessly
  But rushed to him to cover him with kisses,
  Maddened with love as Helen once was maddened.

460 CHRISTIAN.   But—

ROXANE.   I read your letters, reread, re-reread them,
  Saddened by my unworthiness, but gladdened
  By the knowledge that you, like Jupiter,
  Had descended to me, a hapless Semele,
  Your words all golden petals. The flower that shed them
465 Your soul, a soul afire with sincerity.

CHRISTIAN.   The sincerity—that came across then?

ROXANE.   Oh,
  My cross is the cross of my stupidity.
  My soul sinks to its knees, from which, I know,
  Your love will raise me. But the heart that lies
470 Crushed by love's burden cannot be raised. It cries:
  'Forgive me, dearest. Let me veil my eyes
  In anguish. Tell me how I can atone

For the sin that lies upon me like a stone—
The insult of loving you for your beauty alone.'

CHRISTIAN. [*desperately perturbed.*]
475   Heavens!

ROXANE.   Later I learned, just as a bird
Learns how to soar, to feel my spirit stirred
By the totality of you, flesh and soul,
Loving the two together. But the goal
Of true love should be elsewhere—

CHRISTIAN. [*frightened.*]   What do you
480   Love now?

ROXANE.   [*ecstatically.*]
           You, the essential you, the true
Free being hidden by the casual dress
Of flesh I loved you for at first. I can guess
What torture it was for a great soul like yours
To see love lavished on mere caricatures
485   Of your true self—the eyes, the lips, the hair—
But then, with wisdom, with most patient care,
You showed me that in words, *your* words, the key
Lay that would lay bare your heart. I see
That first fair specious image now no more.

CHRISTIAN. [*muttering.*]
490   I don't like this one bit—

ROXANE.   What I loved before
Was a mere bauble. Now I love a soul.

CHRISTIAN.   I'd rather be loved as people usually are—
With a bit of body as well—

ROXANE.   Here, then, the crux:
Henceforth I shall find distraction in your looks
495   Your beauty is a barrier to you.
If you were ugly, twisted all askew,
Dwarfish, deformed, I feel, I *know* I should
Be able to love you more. The greater good
Needs not the lesser good.

CHRISTIAN. [*wretchedly.*]   It was good enough
500   Before.

ROXANE.   Tear off your beauty with a rough
Rude hand, learn an unwonted ugliness

And see how my love shines—

CHRISTIAN.   Ugly?

ROXANE.   Ah yes,
I swear it, ugly.

[*CHRISTIAN turns his back on her, faced with a terrible decision.*]

CHRISTIAN.   Leave me.

ROXANE.   [*astonished.*]   Leave you?

CHRISTIAN.   Just
For a moment. I've some thinking to do. And you must
505   Warm my friends—with a smile—before they—

ROXANE.   Dear Christian, dear dear Christian—

[*And she goes up to the parapet to converse with the* CADETS, *who are getting their muskets ready.* CYRANO, *seeing she has gone, looks out of his tent.* CHRISTIAN *speaks to him.* CYRANO *comes on.*]

CHRISTIAN.   And so I
Know where I stand. You heard?

[*CYRANO nods.*]

                                    She doesn't love
Me any more.

CYRANO.   Stop that, Christian.

CHRISTIAN.   It's *you*.
She loves my soul. You are my soul.

CYRANO.   Too true.

510   **CHRISTIAN.**   And you love her.

CYRANO.   I?

CHRISTIAN.   I know.

CYRANO.   [*quietly, after a pause.*]   That too
Is true.

CHRISTIAN.   Madly.

CYRANO.   More.

CHRISTIAN.   Tell her.

CYRANO.   No.

CHRISTIAN.   Why not?

CYRANO.   Look at me!

CHRISTIAN.   Oh yes, ugly. Ugliness is what
   She wants. She wants me to be ugly.

CYRANO.   Yes.
   I heard. Can you blame me if I bless the thought?
515   But *you* mustn't believe it, you must not
   Believe she wishes you to—

CHRISTIAN. [*emphatically.*]   Let her choose.
   Tell her everything.

CYRANO.   Not this cross, this gallows—

CHRISTIAN.   Cyrano, look at me. I'm a nonentity
   Cursed with a pretty face. Must I destroy
520   Your happiness for that?

CYRANO.   And this mere trickery
   Of words I have, because of that—

CHRISTIAN.   Go back
   With her. Love her. You deserve it. Joy,
   You deserve it. God, I'm on the rack
   With being my own rival. I want to be—

CYRANO.   Come—

525   **CHRISTIAN.**   Loved for what I am, comely and dumb,
   Or else not loved at all. Can't you see,
   Clever as you are, that basic simplicity?
   As for our marriage—that was a fraud—
   Clandestine—unrecorded—and, dear Lord,
530   Unconsummated. Two beds. Both cold.

CYRANO.   Get thee behind me. It will hold
   Till doomsday. After. This whole discussion is
   Academic. We're both going to die.

CHRISTIAN.   No! You must live. As for dying, that's my
535   Duty now.

CYRANO.   You're being obstinate.

CHRISTIAN.   For what I
   Am, or not at all. I'm going to see
   What's happening there. Talk to her. Let her
   Choose.

CYRANO.   I know what her choice will be—
   You.

CHRISTIAN.　I suppose I can hope. Roxane!

CYRANO.　　　　　　　　　　　　　　　　No, no.

ROXANE.　[coming down.]
540　　What is it?

CHRISTIAN.　Cyrano has something to say—
Important.

[He goes up to the parapet and takes his musket.]

ROXANE.　Important? Oh, he's gone.
I seem to have said something to upset him.

CYRANO.　I know what you have said. Did you mean what you said?
Don't be afraid of saying it to me.
545　　Even if he were ugly?

ROXANE.　　　　　　　　　　Even if he—

[Gunfire begins. The CADETS go into battle, including CHRISTIAN.]

CYRANO.　Ah, they've started. Terribly ugly?

ROXANE.　　　　　　　　　　　　　　Terribly.

CYRANO.　Twisted? Deformed? Grotesque?

ROXANE.　　　　　　　　　　　　How could he be
Anything but noble, sublime, great-souled?

CYRANO.　　　　　　　　　　　　　　You'd still
Love him?

ROXANE.　All the more.

CYRANO.　　　　　　　　　God, is it possible
550　　After all? Possible? Roxane, listen to me.

[But LE BRET rushes on and up to CYRANO. He whispers something.]

CYRANO.　No.

ROXANE.　　　　What? What's happening?

CYRANO.　　　　　　　　　　　　　　I can never
Say it now. Finished.

ROXANE.　　　　　　　You were going to
Tell me something.

CYRANO.　　　　　　　Something. Yes. Whatever
It was doesn't matter now. Here's something new
555　　To tell you. Christian—this I swear because
It's God's own truth—was a great soul.

ROXANE. [*agitated.*]   Was?
 You say *was?* Aaaaah—

CYRANO.   It's over.

[CADETS *bring in the dying* CHRISTIAN *and lay him gently down.* ROXANE *runs to him.*]

ROXANE.   Christian!

LE BRET.   He
 Was first over the parapet. The first shot
 Got him.

CARBON.   They're attacking! Come on—steady—
560   Muskets! Cannon!

ROXANE   Christian!

[CYRANO *speaks quietly to* CHRISTIAN *while* ROXANE *sobs.*]

CYRANO.   I told her everything.
 It's you she loves.

CHRISTIAN.   Roxane!

CARBON.   Measure your fireline! Fire! Bayonets ready!

[*We hear the shattering noise of the guns.*]

ROXANE.   Speak, my love—

CARBON.   Charge!

ROXANE.   He's not dead? Speak,
 My love, my love. I feel his cheek
565   Cold against mine—A letter here—for me.

[*She takes the letter from* CHRISTIAN'*s bosom.*]

CYRANO.   My letter—Roxane, I must go. They need me. See.

ROXANE.   Stay awhile. He's dead. You were his friend,
 The only one to know his greatness.

CYRANO.   Yes,
 Roxane.

ROXANE.   He was a great soul, wasn't he?

570   CYRANO.   Yes, Roxane.

ROXANE.   Genius, nobility, no end
 To his magnificence of spirit. Purity,
 Such depth of heart, such tenderness.

CYRANO.   Yes, Roxane.

ROXANE. And now—and now—gone.

[*She weeps bitterly.*]

575 **CYRANO.** And I must die today, knowing that she,
Unknowing, weeps for him but mourns for me.

DE GUICHE. [*off.*]
The signal! Reinforcements coming! Hang on!

ROXANE. On this letter—his blood—his tears—

VOICE. Surrender!

CADETS. No!

ROXANE. His—brave blood. His—tender—
Tears—

[*She faints. RAGUENEAU, who has been cowering under the coach, runs to her. The tigers have made themselves scarce.*]

RAGUENEAU. This battle—suicide—

CYRANO. Get her away.
580 I'm going to lead the charge.

[*DE GUICHE staggers on, with an arm wound.*]

You've proved your
Valour, monsieur. Now do what you have to do—
Get her away.

DE GUICHE. I'll get her away. If you
Can hang on here awhile, we'll win.

[*ROXANE comes to. She staggers off with DE GUICHE and RAGUENEAU.*]

CYRANO. We'll see.
Goodbye, Roxane.

[*CARBON totters on, wounded.*]

CARBON. We're falling back. I got two
585 Hits in the shoulder—

CYRANO. [*calling encouragement.*]
Reculez pas! Hardi!
Drollos! Don't worry. I
Have two deaths to avenge—Christian—my
Happiness.

[*He raises the pike with ROXANE's handkerchief on it.*]

And so fly high,

Little flag. *Tombé dessus! Escrasas tous!*
590   Pipe, piper.

[*BERTRANDOU bravely shrills on his flute.*]

FIRST CADET.   They're coming over!

CYRANO.   Let them. Fire!
      Fire! Fire! Charge!

[*The banner of Imperial Spain appears over the parapet. A* SPANISH OFFICER *appears.*]

SPANISH OFFICER.   Who
      Are these men so anxious to be killed?

CYRANO.   [*firing on him.*]
      These are the Gascony cadets,
      Captain Castel-Jaloux's their chief—
595   Barons who scorn mere baronets—
      These are the Gascony cadets—

[*The rest is lost in the noise of the battle.*]

[*CURTAIN.*]

Act 5

A convent garden

[*It is fifteen years later—1655. The large garden of the Convent of the Ladies of the Cross in Paris is rich in autumn foliage. A flight of stone steps leads up to the gate. In the centre of the stage is a great tree set in the centre of a small oval space. To the left is the conventual house. To the right, a stone bench. Up right, a chapel. In front of the bench there is a sewing frame, beside it a small chair. In a basket there are skeins of silk and wool. The tapestry in the frame in unfinished. NUNS are coming and going across the garden. Some seat themselves on the bench with MOTHER MARGUÉRITE DE JÉSUS. Leaves fall. The NUNS sing an autumn carol.*]

	NUNS.	Around comes the autumn,
		The swallows are leaving,
		The year is unweaving
		Its garment of red.
5		Out of his hiding
		The winter is riding,
		So Nature lies still
		And pretends to be dead.
		Aspen and yew
10		Will be quivering and bare.
		What will we do?
		We'll be shivering the air
		With a round
		Will come Christmas,
15		The feast of the stranger,
		The beasts in the manger
		Will fall on their knees.
		Green in the cloister
		And green on the altar,
20		A promise that green
		Will return to the trees.

[*SISTER MARTHE, who first speaks, was formerly the duenna of ROXANE.*]

SISTER MARTHE.   Sister Claire admired her new coif in the mirror.
Twice.

MOTHER MARGUÉRITE.   Less a sin than an aesthetic error.
Very plain.

SISTER CLAIRE.   That's one tale. Here's another.
25   Sister Marthe is a thief, Reverend Mother.
She stole a plum from the plum pie when the cook
Had her back turned.

SISTER MARTHE.   It was a very small plum.

SISTER CLAIRE.   My look in the mirror was a very small look.

SISTER MARTHE.   Two looks.

MOTHER MARGUÉRITE.   Monsieur de Bergerac's due to come.
30   This evening. It will grieve him to hear of your sins.

SISTER MARTHE.   Please don't do that. You know he'll make fun of us.

SISTER CLAIRE.   He'll say that nuns are greedy.

SISTER MARTHE.   Frivolous.

MOTHER MARGUÉRITE.   [*smiling.*]
Also good. However sternly he begins,
He always ends by saying nuns are good.
35   Good.

SISTER CLAIRE.   It must be ten or a dozen
Years since he started his Saturday visits.

MOTHER MARGUÉRITE.   More.
He's been visiting us ever since his cousin
Came here to live. Fifteen years since that sore
Sad loss of hers. She brought her widow's weeds—
40   As he puts it—to offset our virgin lilies.
He's very poetical. A black dove,
He once said, among grounded seagulls.

SISTER CLAIRE.   His skill is
All in worldly things. Was he ever in love,
I wonder? Such a gentleman, yet he leads
45   A very aggressive life. Once he said to me
That there's a kind of panache in virgin vows.
What did he mean?

MOTHER MARGUÉRITE.   The white plume of celibacy.

He made a rhyme about it.

SISTER MARTHE. He was always witty.
He's the only one who can make her smile.

MOTHER MARGUÉRITE. Very droll.
50   He likes our cake too.

SISTER CLAIRE. It's such a pity
He's not a good Catholic.

SISTER MARTHE. We'll convert him in time.

MOTHER MARGUÉRITE. [*severely.*]
No, I forbid you to meddle with his soul.
He may stop coming here.

SISTER MARTHE. But how about God?

MOTHER MARGUÉRITE. Rest easy. God, being omniscient,
55   Knows all about Monsieur de Bergerac.

SISTER MARTHE. There's not one Saturday I haven't heard him say:
'Ah, dear sister—' And in a proud sort of way,
Too. 'Dear sister—I ate meat yesterday.'

MOTHER MARGUÉRITE. Really? I'd be more ready for praise than
blame
60   If he was telling the truth. The last time he came,
He hadn't eaten for three days.

SISTER CLAIRE. Oh, no.

MOTHER MARGUÉRITE. He's poor, very poor.

SISTER MARTHE. Who told you so?

MOTHER MARGUÉRITE. Monsieur Le Bret.

SISTER CLAIRE. Apart from things like
prayer,
65   Why doesn't somebody help him?

MOTHER MARGUÉRITE. Nobody dare.

[*Upstage, on a tree-lined path,* ROXANE *can be seen, widow-capped, long-veiled.*
DE GUICHE, *grown magnificently old, is with her. They walk slowly.* MOTHER
MARGUÉRITE *rises.*]

We'd better go in. She has a visitor.

SISTER MARTHE.
The Duc de Grammont, as he is now.

SISTER CLAIRE. The Marshal, is it?

SISTER MARTHE.   A long time since he came to call on her.

SISTER CLAIRE.   He's busy, I suppose. The court—the camp—
70   The world—

[*She shudders at that last word. The* NUNS *go in.* ROXANE *and* DE GUICHE *come down in silence, stopping near the embroidery frame.*]

DE GUICHE.   A long time. Too long. God knows
How you can bring yourself to cheat men's eyes
Of all that golden beauty. You propose
To stay here for ever, in mourning?

ROXANE.   For ever.

DE GUICHE.   Ever
Faithful?

ROXANE.   Faithful. My future lies
75   Among the faithful.

DE GUICHE.   Have you forgiven me?

ROXANE.   I'm here. That has to mean I've forgiven you.

DE GUICHE.   Christian—was he really so—?

ROXANE.   If you knew him.

DE GUICHE.   I didn't know him. I didn't particularly
Want to know him. That last letter of his—
80   Do you still wear it next to your—

ROXANE.   Still and for ever.
Like a sacred relic.

DE GUICHE.   I'll never understand
Such a sterile devotion.

ROXANE.   But to me
He isn't really dead. It's as if we
Still meet in some special region, sustained
85   Only by love—not devotion—living love,
Love between the living.

DE GUICHE.   Do you see much of
The other man?

ROXANE. [*lighting up.*]
                    Cyrano? Oh yes, he pays
A weekly visit, acts as my gazette,
My court circular, out on Saturdays.
90   Under that tree, if the weather's fine, they set

A chair for him. I wait with my embroidery.
At four o'clock the clock strikes,
And on the last stroke I hear his step
And his stick tapping the stone steps. He's so
95   Regular, I never turn to see.
First, he laughs at me for what he likes
To call my Penelope web, and, after, he
Retails the chronicle of the week, and—

[*LE BRET, ageing, in an old coat, appears, unhappy.*]

                                          There's Le Bret.
Le Bret, how's our friend?

LE BRET.   Not well, not well at all.

ROXANE.   [*to DE GUICHE.*]
100   He's exaggerating.

LE BRET.   It's just as I say,
Just as I've always said—loneliness,
Wretchedness. He writes those satires of his,
Determined to make more and more enemies.
He attacks false saints, false nobles, false heroes,
105   Plagiaristic poets—in fact, more or less
Everyone. That's no life for anyone.

ROXANE.   Everyone goes
In terror of that sword of his, that's one thing.
No one dares touch him.

DE GUICHE.   [*doubtfully.*]   That may be so.

LE BRET.   Oh, it isn't the violence I fear—it's this loneliness,
110   As I said. It's hunger, poverty, ravening
December with wolves at its heels battering
The door of his dark hovel. Soon they'll catch
Our swordsman off his guard. Every day, you know,
He has to tighten his belt by one more notch.
115   Even his poor old nose isn't the same—
It's like discoloured ivory. And he has only
One rusty, rotting black serge coat to his name.

DE GUICHE.   [*with referred stoicism.*]
This is the world. This is how the world goes.
He takes what comes. Don't pity him too much.

LE BRET.   [*smiling bitterly.*]
120   My lord marshal—

DE GUICHE.   [*firmly.*]   Don't pity him, I say. He
        Lives his life as he wants, he's one of those
        Rare animals that have opted to be free.

LE BRET.   My lord duke—

DE GUICHE.   I know. I have everything. And
        He has nothing, save that one thing. Nevertheless,
125   I think I'd be proud to shake him by the hand.
        Now I have to go.

ROXANE.   I'll go with you
        As far as the gate.

[*DE GUICHE salutes LE BRET and turns with ROXANE towards the steps. They start to climb it. Then he turns to LE BRET.*]

DE GUICHE.   I think I envy him, yes,
        Envy him. There's such a thing as success
        Which sickens like excess. When a man wins
130   The big prizes—having no glaring sins
        To reproach himself with, filling the foreground up—
        He feels sinful nevertheless, defiled from top
        To toe—not with remorse, remorse is too
        Considerable a thing—rather as though
135   Under the silk, under the velvet and ermine,
        There crawled a vague disquieting breed of vermin
        Unknown to moral entomologists.
        Pride bloats to more pride; power never rests.
        The ducal robe sweeps up the endless stair
140   With a dry rustle of dead illusions, a sere
        Whistle of regrets. Just as your veil there,
        Trailing as you mount this literal stair,
        Draws a whisper of dead leaves along.

ROXANE.   I must say
        The sentiment does you honour.

DE GUICHE.   Yes? Le Bret!
        [*To ROXANE.*]
145   Permit us—a brief word.

[*He goes down to LE BRET and speaks quietly.*]

                            It's true. No one
        Dares to attack your friend, not openly.
        But hate grows, and hate will find its way.
        I think you ought to warn him. The other day

At court, one of his haters said to me:
150   'De Bergerac may die—accidentally.'

LE BRET.   I see.

DE GUICHE.   I hope you see. Tell him to stay
At home. To be careful.

LE BRET.   Careful! Whatever I say,
He treads his own path. He's coming here today.
All right, I'll warn him, but—

ROXANE.   [*on the step, to a* NUN *who approaches her.*]
                        Yes, what is it?

155   **NUN.**   This man Ragueneau would like a word with you,
Madame.

ROXANE.   Very well. Bring him to me.
[*To* DE GUICHE *and* LE BRET.]   I suppose
He's come for sympathy—something to warm him on
His long cold downward road. The things he's done—
Pastrycook, poet, singer—

LE BRET.   Bathhouse attendant—

160   **ROXANE.**   Actor—

LE BRET.   Parish beadle—

ROXANE.   Hairdresser—

LE BRET.   Teacher of guitar.

ROXANE.   Poor man—his fortunes always in the descendant.
What next, I wonder.

[RAGUENEAU *comes in hurriedly, agitated. His fatness is clothed in miserable grey.*]

RAGUENEAU.   Dear madame. Your grace.

ROXANE.   [*smiling.*]
First tell your trouble, if troubles they are,
To Monsieur Le Bret.

RAGUENEAU.   But madame—

[ROXANE's *smile forbids further speech. She mounts the stair with* DE GUICHE. RAGUENEAU *comes down to* LE BRET.]

165   I suppose, after all—I mean—in any case,
It's not the sort of thing that—not yet,
Anyhow—

LE BRET.   What, man?

RAGUENEAU.   I went to see him just now,
Our friend, I mean—he was just coming out
Of his lodgings. I hurried on to meet him, but
170   He was walking quickly. At the corner of the street
There's this upper window—he was passing under it—
I wonder if it could really have been
An accident—I wonder—anyway, oh my God,
A servant, a big hairy lout, he let
175   A chunk of wood drop, a great heavy log fall,
Fall—

LE BRET.
        On top of—oh no—

RAGUENEAU.   A massive chuck of wood.

LE BRET.   What are you trying to tell me?

RAGUENEAU.   He was lying there.
I ran up to him as quickly as I could.
A great gash in his—

LE BRET.   Dead?

RAGUENEAU.   Just about alive.
180   I carried him up to his room. Have you seen it? I've
Never seen such—squalor. Oh, my God.

LE BRET.   Is he suffering?

RAGUENEAU.   I don't think so. I don't think he feels
Anything.

LE BRET.   Did you get a—

RAGUENEAU.   A doctor came, yes, out of charity.

LE BRET.   God help him. We mustn't tell her. She
185   Mustn't know, not yet. What did he say,
This doctor—what did he—?

RAGUENEAU.   Technicalities—
Meningeal fever. Lesion of the
Something or other. Oh, if you'd seen him,
Lying there—blood—bandages—
190   But you will now, of course, right away.
We must go quickly. He's all by himself there.
If he tries to get up, and he will, I know he will—
He may, he may—

LE BRET.   [*drawing him to the right.*]
　　　Through the chapel—that's the shortest way—

[*ROXANE appears on the stairway and calls* LE BRET *as he and* RAGUENEAU *hurry to the chapel.*]

195　**ROXANE.**　Monsieur Le Bret!

[*But the two go off without responding.*]

　　　　　　　　　　　Going off when I call him?
　　　Ragueneau, poor man, must have been unusually
　　　Pathetic.

[*She comes slowly down.*]

　　　　　　　This last September day
　　　Makes my old sorrow smile. It's as though
　　　April had come to golden maturity,
200　　So that the fall is really the fall of spring,
　　　A gentle end the mirror of a gentle beginning.

[*She sits down to her embroidery.* SISTERS MARTHE *and* CLAIRE *bring an armchair and place it under the tree.*]

　　ROXANE.　The old chair, for my old friend.

　　SISTER MARTHE.　　　　　　　　　The best of all
　　　The chairs in our parlour.

　　ROXANE.　　　　　　Thank you.

[*They leave. She sews. The clock strikes.*]

　　　　　　　　　　　So. The last stroke.
　　　The hour. This is strange. He was
205　　Never late before. Perhaps the nun
　　　Who's always trying to convert him is trying again.
　　　[*A pause.*]
　　　I've never known him to be as late as this.
　　　He ought to be converted by now.

　　SISTER MARTHE.　[*appearing on the steps.*]
　　　　　　　　　　　　　Here he is,
　　　Madame.
　　　[*More formally.*]
　　　　　　Monsieur de Bergerac.

　　ROXANE.　[*following her old custom of not turning her head to greet him.*]
　　　　　　　　　　　　　　　These
210　　Old faded colours—difficult to match them.

[*She embroiders.* CYRANO, *very pale, his hat over his eyes, appears at the top of the stairway. The* NUN *goes away, troubled by his appearance. He comes down the steps leaning on his stick, keeping upright only by a visible effort.* ROXANE *speaks to him in friendly banter.*]

ROXANE.   Late for the first time, Cyrano—
    After fifteen years.

[CYRANO *reaches his seat with difficulty, his cheerful tone in terrible contrast to his tortured face.*]

CYRANO.   Forgive me, please.
    I was detained, I'm afraid.

ROXANE.   Well?

CYRANO.   By an unexpected visitor.

ROXANE.   [*carelessly, working away.*]
                            Was it a
215   Tiresome visitor?

CYRANO.   Very tiresome.

ROXANE.   And you sent him away?

CYRANO.   For the time being. 'This is Saturday,'
    I said. 'And on Saturday I have a
    Regular engagement. Do me the favour
    Of returning in an hour or so.'

220   ROXANE.   He'll have to wait some time. I shan't let you go
    Before dark.

CYRANO [*gently.*]
                It's just possible, I'm afraid,
    I may have to go before it's dark. My apologies.

[*He leans back wearily in his chair.* SISTER CLAIRE *appears, ostensibly to cut some parsley.*]

ROXANE.   You're neglecting your duties, Cyrano. Here is
    Someone waiting to be teased.

CYRANO.   [*opening eyes he has wearily shut.*]
                            Ah, yes.
225   Come here, sister. You of the beautiful
    Downcast eyes—

[*The* NUN, *approaching according to the comic tradition she has established with* CYRANO, *raises those eyes and is shocked by* CYRANO's *face.* CYRANO *urgently indicates that she must not betray her shock to* ROXANE.]

I have something to confess.
I ate meat again yesterday. Isn't that terrible?

SISTER CLAIRE.   Terrible. And as a penance you must come
To the refectory later and have a nice big bowl
230   Of bouillon.

CYRANO.   I'll be there.

SISTER CLAIRE.   You're becoming quite reasonable,
Monsieur.

ROXANE.   At last you're breaking his obstinate soul.
Now is the time to convert him.

SISTER CLAIRE.   Oh, no, no,
That's something I mustn't do.

CYRANO.   True. And something
You've never, in all these years, tried to do.
235   Bursting with virtue like a spiritual plum,
And yet you never preach. Astonishing.
But now, sister, I'm going to astonish *you*.
I'm going to let you pray for me.

ROXANE.   Look at her—

CYRANO.   Tonight at vespers.

ROXANE.   Struck absolutely dumb.

240   **SISTER CLAIRE.**   You forgot one advantage of my calling, Monsieur.
I can pray without permission. And I will.

[*She goes off, troubled.* CYRANO *turns to* ROXANE, *bending over her work.*]

CYRANO.   Patient Penelope is weaving still.
There's one thing everyone can be sure about
And that is that, alas, I'll never see
245   How that piece of work eventually turns out.

ROXANE.   [*smiling.*]
I wondered how long it would be
Before you said that.

[*A flurry of wind sends some leaves down.*]

CYRANO.   The year unweaves
Her tapestry. Look at them.

ROXANE.   Such colour.
Perfect Venetian red. They're falling fast.

250 CYRANO.   They fall well. With a sort of panache.
They plume down in their last
Loveliness, disguising their fear
Of being dried and pounded to ash
To mix with the common dust.
255 They go in grace, making their fall appear
Like flying.

ROXANE.   You're melancholy today.

CYRANO.   Never. I'm not the melancholy sort.

ROXANE.   Very well, then. We'll let
The leaves of the fall fall while you
260 Turn the leaves of my gazette.
What's new at court?

CYRANO.   Let me see, let me see.
Saturday the nineteenth. His Majesty
Was ill after eating too much preserved ginger—
Eight helpings, to be precise. The court's decree
265 Was that it was high treason so to injure
The royal viscera. So there and then
The offending ginger was condemned to death,
And the royal pulse slowed to normal again.
What next? Ah yes, Sunday the twentieth.
270 The Queen gave a great ball, and they burned
Seventeen hundred and sixty-three wax candles.
A minor item: our army, so it's learned,
Has been victorious in Austria. There have been some scandals
To do with witches. A bishop went to heaven,
275 Or so it's believed: there's been as yet no report
Of his arrival. Madame d'Athis's dog, a sort
Of hairier smaller Madame d'Athis, was given
An enema—

ROXANE.   Monsieur de Bergerac, that will do.

CYRANO.   Monday, the twenty-first—nothing. Lygdamire
280 Has a new lover.

ROXANE.   [indicating that this is always happening.]
            Oh.

CYRANO.   Tuesday, the twenty-second,
The entire court removed to Fontainebleau.
Wednesday: the Comte de Fiesque unequivocally beckoned

To Madame de Montglat. It's believed that she said no.
Thursday, La Mancini was Queen of France,
285   Or very nearly. Friday, during a dance,
Madame de Montglat, so the rumours go,
Said yes. Saturday, the twenty-sixth—

[*He closes his eyes. His head falls. Silence.* ROXANE, *surprised, turns, looks, is frightened, rises, goes towards him.*]

    ROXANE.   Cyrano!

    CYRANO.   [*opening his eyes.*]
                Yes? What? What is it?

[*He sees* ROXANE *bending over him. He quickly pulls down his hat over his face, leaning away from her.*]

                                It's nothing,
Nothing at all. I shall be all right. Just
290   My old wound from Arras. It likes to sting
Sometimes, to remind me that it's still there.

    ROXANE.   My poor dear friend.

    CYRANO.   It doesn't last.
It will go soon. There—it's gone.

[*He forces a smile.*]

    ROXANE.   [*standing near him.*]   We all of us
Have our old wounds. Mine is here—on yellowing
295   Paper, bloodstained, tearstained, hardly legible.

    CYRANO.   His letter. Didn't you say that, one day,
You'd let me read it?

[*Twilight begins to fall.*]

    ROXANE.   You want to? You really
Want to?

    CYRANO.   Yes. Today. Now.

    ROXANE.   Take it, then.

[*She gives him the little bag from around her neck.*]

    CYRANO.   I may open it?

    ROXANE.   Open it. Read it.

[*She goes back to her embroidery, folding it, arranging the silk. But* CYRANO *does not open the letter.*]

CYRANO. 'Goodbye

300 Roxane. For this is the last time I
Shall be able to write—'

ROXANE. [*surprised.*] Aloud?

CYRANO. 'I have to die
Some time today. My beloved, how
Heavy my heart is, and it is heavy too
With so great a burden of love, love still untold,
305 Perhaps unguessed at, unprospected gold
From love's new world, not to be mined, for now
The time for its shining forth is gone, all gone.
Never more shall my eyes kiss the sight of you,
The flight of your gestures. I think of one—
310 The way you have of pushing back a strand
Of your hair from your forehead—and
My heart wants to cry out—'

ROXANE. You read it,
You read it in such a way—

[*The night is approaching.*]

CYRANO. 'But now I can only cry:
Goodbye, my dearest—'

ROXANE. In such a voice—

CYRANO. 'Goodbye,
315 My angel, my heart's treasure, my one love—'

ROXANE. A voice, I know, I am not hearing for
The first time, speaking such words—

CYRANO. 'Never for one second has my heart
Been absent from your presence. And, as the night
320 Deepens, the shadows of the next world start
To close in on me, I shall be that one
Whose love, raging and blessing like the sun
That outlives all men, will live on and on
Beyond the sun's limits—'

ROXANE. How can you
325 Possibly read now—in this lack of light?

[*She has risen and gone to him. He opens his eyes, notices, makes a gesture of surprise, almost of fear, then bows his head. There is a long pause. Then, in a darkness still growing, she speaks slowly, hands clasped.*]

For all of fifteen years you have played the role
Of the old friend, affectionate, droll,
But never one hint of—

CYRANO. Roxane—

ROXANE. So it was you.

CYRANO. Oh no, Roxane, no, no—

ROXANE. I might
330   Have known, every time you spoke my name.

CYRANO. Not I, oh no—

ROXANE. It was you.

CYRANO. Roxane, I swear—

ROXANE. I see through it all now—that generous
Imposture—the letters—it was you.

CYRANO. No.

ROXANE. It was always you. The mad, dear
335   Foolish words—

CYRANO. No.

ROXANE. The voice in the night,
You.

CYRANO. Upon my honour.

ROXANE. It was all
And always you.

CYRANO. I never loved you.

ROXANE. You
Loved me.

CYRANO. It was he who loved you.

ROXANE. Even
Now you love me.

CYRANO. [*feebly.*] No.

340 **ROXANE.** That *no* is not so strong
As it was a second or two ago.

CYRANO. No, no, my dear love.
I never loved you.

ROXANE. And all these fifteen long years,
While you stayed silent, you knew, you knew

345   That his letter was stained by *your* tears,
     Not—

    CYRANO.   His blood, though, stained by his blood.

    ROXANE.   And you
     Never said, never hinted, never once. Why
     Do you break silence now?

    CYRANO.   [*confused and weary.*]   Oh, because I—

[*LE BRET and RAGUENEAU come running in.*]

    LE BRET.   This will be your last madness. How could you
350   Be so—
     [*To RAGUENEAU.*]
     He's here.

    CYRANO.   [*smiling, trying to rise.*]
              Yes indeed, I am here.

    LE BRET.   You ought to know,
     Madame, that he's killed himself to come to you.

    ROXANE.   Oh my God, that faintness—I wondered—

    CYRANO.   I regret
     That I rudely intermitted my gazette.
355   On Saturday, the twenty-sixth, an hour before
     Dinner, Monsieur de Bergerac
     Was foully, ignobly
     Murdered.

[*He takes off his hat and shows the bandages swathing his head.*]

    ROXANE.   [*desperately.*]
              Cyrano, what have they done to you?

    CYRANO.   At Arras, I said I wanted to depart
360   With honourable steel piercing my heart
     And a piercing epigram upon my lips.
     That's what I said. But fate's a great buffoon,
     A balloon-pricker, a deflater of the most stoic
     Postures, a specialist in traps and trips.
365   Look at me—ambushed, taken in the rear
     In a gutter for a battlefield, my heroic
     Foe a scullion, his weapon a mere
     Firelog. My life has played a consistent tune.
     I've missed everything—even death.

    RAGUENEAU.   [*breaking down.*]   Oh, monsieur—

370   **CYRANO.**   Don't blubber, Ragueneau, my fellow poet.
       Poets should be dry-eyed. Cease your sobs
       And tell me what you're writing these days.

[*He takes* RAGUENEAU'S *hand.*]

       RAGUENEAU.   Nothing. All I do is odd menial jobs
       For Molière.

       CYRANO.   Oh, Molière.

       RAGUENEAU.   Yes, but I'm leaving the swine
375   Tomorrow. Yesterday they played *Scapin,*
       His new comedy. He's stolen a whole scene
       From you.

       LE BRET.   That's true: the one with the great line:
       '*Que diable allait-il faire en cette galère?*'

       RAGUENEAU.   I could murder him.

       CYRANO.   [*evenly.*]   When a poet has taste he can
       show it
380   By stealing from his betters. I gather his play's
       A success?

       RAGUENEAU.   Your scene was. The audience laughed
       And laughed and laughed—

[*The memory makes him cry.*]

       CYRANO.   [*with rancour.*]   My life—all of a piece—a shaft
       Of sun, a puff of air, and then not even
       A memory. Roxane—do you recall
385   That night—the balcony, the ivied wall,
       Christian? I stood in the shadows, underneath,
       And left it to another to climb and claim
       The kiss of glory. It happened again and again—
       The shadow for me, for others the applause, the fame.
390   There's a kind of justice somewhere. Even in the teeth
       Of what's to come I can say: Gentlemen,
       Take down this truism in your commonplace books:
       Molière has genius; Christian had good looks.

[*The chapel bell is ringing. The* NUNS *proceed to their prayers.*]

       They're going to pray now. Nymphs, in your orisons,
395   Etcetera etcetera—

       ROXANE.   [*calling.*]   Sister, sister!

CYRANO. [*grasping her hand.*]   No.
  Don't go away. When you come back I may
  Not be here.

[*The NUNS have entered the chapel. An organ plays quietly.*]

                    A little defunctive music—
  That's all I need now.

ROXANE.   You must live.
  I love you.

CYRANO.   Don't say that. That doesn't come
400   Into the story. When the princess said
  I love you to the enchanted prince
  Who was a toad or something, all his ugliness
  Melted away under the sunlight of
  Those words. You magic doesn't work. *Love,*
405   You say. But, as you see, I'm still the same.

ROXANE.   How can I ever forgive myself? It's I
  Who have done this to you—

CYRANO. [*serenely.*]   Let no shred of blame
  Cling to your silk. I never had
  Much acquaintance with the
410   Sweetness of woman. My mother was,
  Understandably perhaps, not pleased
  With what she'd produced. I had no
  Sister. Later, in manhood, I
  Learned to fear the
415   Mistress with mockery in the tail of her eye.
  But—and God bless you for this for ever and ever—
  I have had one friend different from
  The few others.
  A friend in a silken gown in my life.

[*The moon has begun to illuminate the scene. LE BRET points to it.*]

420   LE BRET.   There's another friend.

CYRANO. [*smiling.*]   I see her.

ROXANE. [*heartbroken.*]
  I never loved but one man in my life.
  Now I must lose him twice.

CYRANO.   Le Bret, I shall mount soon to that opaline
    presence, plunge into that crystalline river

425 Or lake of light, without a lunar machine
Or astral rocket—

LE BRET. What are you saying?

CYRANO. The moon.
There are great names up there, other friends—
Socrates, Plato, Galileo—

LE BRET. [*angrily.*] No, no!
I won't have it. It's stupid, it's unjust.
Such a poet, such a great
430 Heart, such a man—to die like this, to die
Like this—

CYRANO. There he goes growling, my
Old bear Le Bret.

LE BRET. My dear dear dear—

[CYRANO's *delirium begins. He half rises, his eyes wandering.*]

CYRANO. We are the Gascony cadets.
Captain Castel-Jaloux—It's a matter of
435 The constitution of the elementary mass.
Yes? The *quidditas* of the *hic*—eh?

LE BRET. Delirious, all that learning—

CYRANO. The testimony
Of Copernicus is worth considering
On that particular point—

ROXANE. [*desperate.*] Oh no—

440 **CYRANO.** *Que diable allait-il faire en cette galère?*
What the devil was he doing or going to do there?

[*He has a moment of clarity. He declaims.*]

Philosopher and scientist,
Poet, musician, duellist,
And voyager through space,
445 A sort of controversialist,
Whose wit kept to a charted track
But sped at a great pace,
A lover too, who seemed to lack
The luck in love of other men—
450 Here lies Hercule-Savinien
De Cyrano de Bergerac,
Nothing, everything, nothing again—

> Sunk now, without a trace.
> I have to leave you. Sorry. I can't stay.
455 That lunar shaft is—waiting to carry me away,
> A punctual and impatient sort of
> Engine.

[He falls back in his chair. The sobbing of ROXANE *recalls him to reality. He looks at her. He strokes her veiled hair.]*

> I would not ask that you mourn any the less
> That good brave Christian blessed with handsomeness,
460 But, when the final cold sniffs at my heart
> And licks my bones, perhaps you might impart
> A double sense to your long obsequies,
> And make those tears, which have been wholly his,
> Mine too, just a little, mine, just a—

465 **ROXANE.**   My love, my only love—

*[*CYRANO, *shaken again by fever and delirium, brusquely raises himself. The others move forward to help him, but he brushes them away. He sets his back against the tree trunk.]*

> **CYRANO.**   Not here, oh no, not lying down. Let
> No one try to help me—only this
> Tree. He's coming. He's coming. Already
> I feel myself being shod in marble,
470 Gloved in lead.
> *[With joy.]*
>   Let him come, then.
> He shall find me on my feet—

[He draws.]

> My sword in my hand.

> **LE BRET.**   Cyrano!

> **CYRANO.**   There he is, looking at me, grinning
475 At my nose. Who is he
> To grin, that noseless one?
> What's that you say—useless, useless?
> You have it wrong, you empty brain pan.
> You see, a man
480 Fights for far more than the mere
> Hope of winning. Better, far better
> To know that the fight is totally
> Irreparably incorrigibly in vain.

A hundred against—no, a thousand.
485   And I recognize every one, every one of you.

[*He lunges at the air again and again.*]

All my old enemies—Falsehood, Compromise,
Prejudice, Cowardice. You ask for my
Surrender? Ah no, never, no, never. Are
You there too, Stupidity?
490   You above all others perhaps were predestined
To get me in the end. But no, I'll
Fight on, fight on, fight—

[*He swings his sword again, then stops breathless. During his last speech he falls into* LE BRET's *arms.*]

You take everything—the rose and the laurel too.
Take them and welcome. But, in spite of you,
495   There is one thing goes with me when tonight
I enter my last lodging, sweeping the bright
Stars from the blue threshold with my salute.
A thing unstained, unsullied by the brute
Broken nails of the world, by death, by doom
500   Unfingered—See it there, a white plume
Over the battle—A diamond in the ash
Of the ultimate combustion—

[ROXANE *kisses his forehead. He opens his eyes, recognizes her, smiles.*]

My panache.

[CURTAIN.]

Related Readings

Alba della Fazia Amoia

The Masterpieces

from
Edmond Rostand

Alba della Fazia Amoia shares some interesting details about the original production of Cyrano de Bergerac *in 1897. The author contrasts the real Cyrano de Bergerac with Rostand's character.*

THE TWO PLAYS that may be characterized as Rostand's most developed and mature works—*Cyrano of Bergerac* and *The Eaglet*—were produced in 1897 and 1900, respectively. The former is the glorious burst of the summer of Rostand's life. The latter was written at the beginning of a painful period of illness, destined to become the author's melancholy autumn.

Cyrano of Bergerac: *A Dream in Action*

In about three and a half centuries of modern theatrical history, there have been recorded in France only two other triumphs comparable to that of Rostand's *Cyrano of Bergerac*: the first was Corneille's *Le Cid*, produced in 1637 during the time of Richelieu;[1] the other, *Le Mariage de Figaro* by Beaumarchais, presented in 1784 in the dawn of the French Revolution.

Cyrano of Bergerac was first produced on December 28, 1897, at the Porte Saint-Martin Theater. Exactly one hour after the curtain had fallen, practically the entire audience was still in the theater applauding. The most curious historic aspect accompanying the play's production was the pessimism that had marked the preparations and rehearsals. Even though the name of Edmond Rostand was well known in turn-of-the-century Paris, the idea of an heroic-comic drama in rhymed alexandrine[2] verse, built on an historic background in the Romantic manner of sixty years earlier, constituted an

---

1. **Richelieu** chief minister of France under King Louis XIII (1624–1642)
2. **alexandrine** iambic line having twelve syllables; standard line in French poetry

anachronism.[3] The Parisian public was sophisticated and demanding, but at the same time seemed to be avid for nothing but Imperial plays and easy *pochades* (light comedies).

The Fleury brothers, who were the directors of the Porte Saint-Martin Theater, after having accepted *Cyrano of Bergerac* for production, regretted it almost immediately afterward. They were pessimistic about its success and felt that if the play ran for a dozen performances, it would be a stroke of luck. In the face of such a negative attitude, it was decided to hold production expenses down to a minimum. Rostand found himself in the predicament of having to pay for the actors' seventeenth-century costumes—in the amount of one hundred thousand francs—out of his own pocket. As for the stage sets, they were so meager that during the dress rehearsal Rostand broke down and was on the verge of assaulting the stage designer. Notwithstanding the famous Constant Coquelin's zeal for the part of the protagonist[4] which was his, pessimism prevailed throughout the theater. One of the members of the company asked Coquelin what his predictions were regarding the play's success; he answered in a single word, shaking his head negatively: "Dark." Instead, that night of December was to mark the beginning of a glorious career on stages throughout the world for the swashbuckling[5] swordsman-poet, Cyrano of Bergerac. Capricious[6] and unpredictable in its reactions, the Parisian theatrical public had nonetheless been able to discern[7] accents of an authentic poetry behind the verbal virtuosity[8] and the visual artifices[9] of the play.

The story of Cyrano is well known in its broad lines. As told by Edmond Rostand, it reveals an ingenuousness[10] and, in many verses, a quixoticism[11] recalling the author's Spanish ancestry. Cyrano is an unvanquished[12] swordsman and an affected,[13] versatile poet, possessed of an enormous, grotesque nose which "arrives so long ahead of him" that it prevents him from giving free rein to his true nature, that of an incurable sentimentalist. He is secretly

---

3. **anachronism** something that is out of its proper time in history
4. **protagonist** main character
5. **swashbuckling** swaggering; boasting; bullying
6. **capricious** impulsive; erratic
7. **discern** recognize
8. **virtuosity** technical skill
9. **artifices** tricks
10. **ingenuousness** originality; cleverness
11. **quixoticism** foolish idealism; chivalry
12. **unvanquished** undefeated
13. **affected** emotionally moved

enamored of[14] his beautiful cousin, Roxane, who in turn loves the young soldier, Christian de Neuvillette, an attractive man but completely devoid of poetry and wit. Roxane, fearful that the gentle Christian, who has just joined the corps of Gascon cadets, will suffer in the hands of his rough and rude fellow soldiers, entrusts him to her cousin, Cyrano. The latter takes his assignment so seriously and conscientiously that he even composes for Christian highly perfected love letters for his beautiful lady. In fact (in one of the most famous scenes of the play), taking advantage of the darkness, he boldly and passionately declares his love to Roxane, who is on the balcony of her home. Cyrano then altruistically[15] withdraws to allow Christian to receive Roxane's kiss. In the meantime, however, the Count de Guiche, commander of the cadets, has also fallen in love with the beautiful Roxane. Unable to stop the marriage of the enamored young couple, he takes his vengeance by sending Christian and Cyrano to besiege the town of Arras. During the siege, Cyrano's passionate correspondence grows more voluminous,[16] and his letters begin to produce a profound change in Roxane, rendering her love deeper and more spiritual. Now she loves Christian no longer for his external beauty but for his soul— that is, she loves Cyrano. Suddenly and unexpectedly, she appears at the Arras military camp, but on that very day, Christian, who now understands that Roxane has unknowingly fallen in love with Cyrano, has decided to tell her the truth about the correspondence. Realizing he is loved for someone else's spirit and intelligence, he voluntarily seeks his death; he is wounded in battle and dies. Cyrano, out of respect for his friend, keeps the secret for fifteen years. On the verge of death resulting from a long illness caused by a falling beam striking his head, Cyrano, in delirium, confesses his long, immutable and unrequited love to the anguished Roxane. Dying, he lifts his sword high, and his last noble, proud words are: "Stainless, unbent, I have kept . . . / . . . My plume! *mon panache.*"

Such is the story that, bursting forth in sonorous[17] verses and in a kaleidoscope of glistening images, has been holding audiences enthralled for almost eighty years. The student who recently declared that, in this age of cosmetic surgery, Cyrano of Bergerac is no longer plausible nor relevant, has, of course, missed the whole point of the play. It is not Cyrano's nose that prevents Roxane from loving him; it is rather the fact that he is not Christian. Even if Cyrano had been endowed with a beautiful nose, Roxane would still not love her cousin. The existence of the handsome Christian, speaking and writing with beauty borrowed from Cyrano's soul, is the image that holds

---

14. **enamored of** filled with love and desire for
15. **altruistically** unselfishly
16. **voluminous** numerous
17. **sonorous** rich and full in sound

Roxane enthralled, and her "pink lip will inevitably tend toward his blond moustache." Roxane does not find Cyrano ugly, but a normal-nosed Cyrano would not satisfy her esthetically either.

And yet the nose is what has immortalized Rostand's character. Famous actors—Constant Coquelin, Ralph Richardson, José Ferrer, Gino Cervi, Jean Piat, Christopher Plummer—their faces disfigured by an enormous false nose, have been acclaimed and will be remembered for their interpretations of Cyrano of Bergerac. In North America, the character was made familiar through the adaptations and stagings of Walter Hampden and Anthony Burgess. Such an abundance and variety of interpretations of the character of Cyrano suggest that part of this study should concern itself with the figure of the real Cyrano, since Rostand's point of departure for the play was the character of an authentic personage who lived in Paris in the seventeenth century during the time of Richelieu and Mazarin.[18]

Before focusing on the real Cyrano, however, it may be of interest to note that as a young boarder at school, Edmond Rostand, already distinguished among his companions for his talent in composition, had offered to write love letters and poems for a friend of his, who copied them over and sent them to his young girlfriend. This personal recollection somehow imposes itself on the chronicles that have created the immortal trio of Cyrano, Christian, and Roxane. Moreover, Rostand's wife, in her book about her husband, relates an anecdote that sheds light on how the first idea came to the dramatist for the writing of *Cyrano of Bergerac*. Rosemonde states that Edmond was spending a summer in the town of Luchon, a resort in the Haute-Garonne, where he happened to meet, beside a fountain, a young man who obviously had been grievously disappointed in love and was nursing his sorrow. Edmond drew out the boy's story, then spoke to him at length, consolingly and paternally. For several days, Amédée returned to the fountain to listen to Edmond's "teachings," after which he disappeared. Rostand was quite triumphant when, some time later, he met the young lady involved and she said to him in a burst of passion: "You know, my little Amédée, whom I had judged to be so mediocre, is marvelous: he's a scholar, a thinker, a poet. . . ." Amédée was, of course, none of these things; he was just a pale reflection of her ideal, but the idea for *Cyrano* was born.

When Rostand submitted his manuscript of *Cyrano of Bergerac* for publication, he inscribed on the first page:

It is to the soul of CYRANO that I wished to dedicate this poem. But since it has entered into you, COQUELIN, it is to you that I dedicate it.

---

18. **Mazarin** French cardinal who succeeded Richelieu as prime minister of France

Coquelin, as has been noted already, was the first actor to portray the role of the poetic swordsman with the long nose. In the light of Rostand's dedication, it is reasonable to ask how much of the soul of the real Cyrano passed on to the stage, and how much from the stage into the legend; or, better yet, to ask why Rostand's imagination was so fired by the figure of a Gascon cadet who died at the age of thirty-six in the most melancholy obscurity.

The first encounter with the real, historic Cyrano is slightly disappointing: the Gascon cadet was, in fact, not a Gascon, even though he served in the company which subsequently became legendary. Savinien de Cyrano (the name given to our hero at the baptismal font) was born in Paris, of Parisian parents, on March 6, 1619, in one of the oldest and most populous neighborhoods of the capital—Les Halles. The family was rather well off, and enjoyed the prestige of a modest title of nobility. His father's name was Abel de Cyrano; the noble particule, de Bergerac, appeared later, following the acquisition of a castle on the outskirts of Paris. There were, in reality, two castles. The first, Mauvières, still exists today, although much transformed by restorations over the last century. The second castle has disappeared; not even its ruins remain. It is known, however, to have been called Bergerac, and was located near the village of the same name (now called Sous-Forêt) in the Chevreuse valley. According to established usage of the time among noble families, Abel's first child, Denyse, was authorized to use the name Cyrano de Mauvières: the second, Savinien, future swordsman and poet, Cyrano de Bergerac. It was probably the suffix -ac that misled Rostand and prompted him to make his hero a Gascon gentleman. Names of families and villages ending in -ac are, in fact, typical of Gascony. It is possible, too, that the original owners of the castle and fief[19] were Gascons.

In accordance with the practices of the time, male offspring were sent to board with churchmen, and female offspring to convents. Savinien was no exception. His early education at Mauvières was entrusted to a country priest, who also had charge of Cyrano's future friend and apologist,[20] the pious Henry Le Bret. At the age of twelve, after five years of what the great Italian dramatist, Count Vittorio Alfieri, a century later, would have defined as "ineducation," Cyrano left the boarding school. He had won a scholarship for the Collège de Beauvais in Paris, where he remained for six years and learned to detest tradition, cultural Aristotelianism, and the constituted authorities which were the mainstays of seventeenth-century society.

At this point in his life appeared the beautiful lady who was destined to become the inspiration for Roxane. In Rostand's play, her name is Madeleine

---

19. **fief** land that can be inherited

20. **apologist** person who writes or speaks in defense of a belief or action

Robin, and she is in love with the handsome Christian de Neuvillette. The real Cyrano de Bergerac did indeed have a cousin with a not dissimilar name: Madeleine Robineau, bourgeoise[21] by birth, but married to a nobleman, the Baron de Neuvillette. Through her marriage in 1635 she had become a member of Parisian high society and stood out conspicuously among the most highly considered ladies. It was she who took charge of Cyrano's social education. It is not known whether the Baroness de Neuvillette was really a *précieuse* like Rostand's Roxane, but it is known that she had two great passions—good food and dancing—and that, like Roxane, she was noted for her "peach complexion." It was in her company that Cyrano learned the usages of high society and the good manners which he sorely lacked. Whether he was enamored of Madeleine is not known. It is certain, however, that he was profoundly influenced by her and found her fascinating.

The relationship, however, was not destined to last long: Cyrano's father, tired of financing his son's follies, decided to pull tight the purse strings, whereupon Cyrano decided to enlist as a cadet with the Noble Guards of the Gascon Captain, Carbon de Casteljaloux, to whom he had been introduced by his ever faithful friend, Le Bret. Cyrano was wounded in battle at Mouzon in 1639; the following year he left the Cadets and became part of the regiment of the Counts, participating in the siege of Arras—a boring affair, as all sieges are. Cyrano and his companions spent their time smoking and playing cards, just as in the opening scene of the fourth act of Rostand's play. The wife of the newlywed young Count of Canvoye was very much in love with her husband, and a graphomaniac[22] besides—she sent him as many as three letters a day. The Count, who was not very gifted as a writer, in order to hide his embarrassment, turned for help on more than one occasion to Cyrano, who supplied him with love poems to send to his beloved wife. It is probably this historic fact that furnished Rostand with the idea for the famous letter substitution by Cyrano for the handsome but almost illiterate Christian.

The boredom of the siege was broken by an enemy attack. Cyrano, in the front line, was stabbed in the throat by an enemy saber. When he regained consciousness in a rudimentary camp infirmary, he learned that among those who had fallen in battle was the Baron de Neuvillette, Madeleine's husband. The death of Christian at Arras is not, therefore, a literary invention, nor is the widow's withdrawal to a convent. When, in fact, Cyrano left the military service and returned home to convalesce in Paris, he learned that Madeleine was spending her life in prayer and penitence. He had the opportunity of seeing her in the Convent of the Holy Cross on the day that

---

21. **bourgeoise** middle-class
22. **graphomaniac** person with an excessive enthusiasm for writing

his sister, Catherine, took the veil.[23] He scarcely recognized Madeleine: her mourning gown was of the poorest sort, her face was devastated by tears and fasting; and the former "peach complexion" was hidden under long gray hair that Madeleine no longer attempted to disguise by artificial coloring. In the face of this manifestation[24] of profound humility, Cyrano experienced a sort of reverse exhibitionism; he fled from the convent, horrified, and vowed never to return.

The ex-Cadet of Gascony now lived as he could, in the intellectual circles of Paris, where he underwent the influence of the famous mathematician and materialist philosopher, Gassendi. Refusing all protectors, he preferred to gain his own reputation for libertine[25] ideas and extravagance. He wrote two fantasies in prose, *Le Voyage dans la lune* and *L'Histoire des Etats de l'Empire du Soleil*, letters, maxims, and even a study of physics. Author also of a comedy (*Le Pédant joué*) and a tragedy (*La Mort d'Agrippine*) that he was unsuccessful in having presented, Cyrano finally was constrained to turn to a protector—Louis, Duke of Arpajon, Marquis of Séverac and Count of Rodez. Notwithstanding the Duke's protection, the presentation of his tragedy was a failure. The audience rioted on the first night because of an innocent line which Cyrano's enemies chose to interpret as a sacrilege.[26] Presentations of the play were suspended and, as a result, requests for the text at the Charles de Sercy publishing house reached an all-time high. The Duke began to regret the protection he had accorded, and Cyrano, too, felt the weight of the attachment. A fortuitous[27] accident—or a plot—hastened their separation: a beam fell from the roof of the ducal[28] residence and struck the poet on the head; he was to remain for a year on the threshold of death. And this is the ambush that is freely evoked by Rostand in the fifth act of his play.

The good Le Bret undertook to have his injured friend transported to the home of a certain Tanneguy for treatment. Madeleine visited him there twice, but her words of comfort apparently must not have been much appreciated, since the dying Cyrano sent word to his cousin, Pierre de Cyrano, who lived in Lannois, begging him to come to fetch him and promising that he would not disturb him for too long—just a few days. Pierre answered the call of distress, arriving at Tanneguy's home on July 25th; Cyrano, wavering, rose from bed, got dressed, went downstairs, and was assisted into

---

23. **took the veil** became a nun
24. **manifestation** clear evidence
25. **libertine** morally unrestrained
26. **sacrilege** disrespectful treatment of something considered sacred
27. **fortuitous** fortunate
28. **ducal** belonging to a duke

the waiting carriage. On July 28, 1655, just a few days later, he was, in fact, dead, in accordance with his promise to his cousin. Cyrano de Bergerac's was a first-class mind whose brilliant fantasies, ingenious scientific hypotheses, and bold religious and political views were prematurely interrupted. Rostand, by reviving him in his celebrated play, contributed much to his fame. Rostand's hero, however, is very different from the real Cyrano, even though many biographical elements in the play are exact and though there are significant similarities between the two figures.

Rostand merely develops the figure of the noble idealist who fights against the reality of ordinary life. His Cyrano, however, never admits to such a reality but creates his own world. In such a personal cosmos, the objective observer might judge him to be the loser, but Cyrano gains for himself his most precious ideal—*panache*. Cyrano's world comprises two existences: the life of each day and the life of love. He cherishes the highest concepts of life and duty; in them are contained the plot of the play and the story of his soul. Rostand dedicated the work to the *soul* of Cyrano. The play is an heroic comedy, which is very close to tragedy. As in a Molière play, not only is the sacrifice of a noble soul seen, but also the struggle of an heroic soul against all the evils of society and even against that love of idealism that can be harmful because of its own strength. From this point of view, Rostand's Cyrano surpasses the real one; love works miracles. It is this love that carries Roxane's soul to a higher level. Cyrano's idealism causes those who approach him to become idealistic, too. But the real tragedy lies in the fact that this idealistic love, which renders Roxane faithful to the memory of Christian, is the source of all of Cyrano's heroism and all his hatred for convention. In the end, it is also the cause of his death. What Cyrano loves so passionately is not Roxane—who, in truth, does not at all deserve his love, at least in the beginning of the play. He loves Love itself. He loves the fantasy that he has invented and which has become his ideal, personified by Roxane. The interest of the play, therefore, lies in the soul of Cyrano. To seize the essence of this great soul and to appreciate the true heroism of the comedy, an analysis of the internal and external figure of Rostand's creation is necessary.

Cyrano may be considered first as an able and clever man with a temperament that, once aroused, can manifest itself sweetly and paternally—but only in intimacy or in a deeply sincere relationship. Usually he is extremely violent. The most important external aspect of his character is the cult[29] of the gesture, of which there are two kinds. First, there is the splendid gesture, the theatrical gesture, the execution of a duel while composing an improvised

---

29. **cult** devoted attachment to a principle or idea

ballad, or marching at the head of a motley[30] procession to fight single-handed against one hundred men. These are bravuras[31] inspired by Cyrano's grotesque external appearance, but he executes them because he is full of life, energy and goodness—and is timid inside. He is a poet and a creator, but he senses his own ugliness and has lost his love for his own life. This explains the splendor of his verses. . . .

In addition to the splendid gestures, there are Cyrano's heroic gestures, which render his soul so noble and great: the letters he writes for Roxane on behalf of Christian; the balcony scene, in which he directs the unfolding of the lovers' exchange all for his friend's benefit. These magnanimous gestures are so much more beautiful than the others because they are completely gratuitous.[32] They are born of Cyrano's own personal pride and of his heroism. Perhaps the best example, however, of the heroic gesture is the scene that so poignantly[33] combines the comic and the tragic: the scene in which Cyrano detains the Count de Guiche from entering Roxane's home, where her marriage ceremony to Christian is being performed—a ceremony that Cyrano wishes desperately would not take place and yet which he desires fervently for his beloved Roxane's happiness. Pretending to fall heavily, as if from a great height, and lying motionless as if stunned by his fall from the moon, Cyrano intercepts the Count's approach and holds him enthralled for the time necessary for Roxane and Christian to plight their troth. . . .

In the heroic gesture may be seen the tragedy of the man of genius: Cyrano is a poet, a philosopher, an indomitable fencer and an idealist; but he is not successful *because* he is heroic, *because* he is idealistic, and *because* he fears ridicule. His philosophy, as he explains it to Le Bret, is: ". . . Let what will befall / Always I will be admirable, in all." The genuine Cyrano is the Cyrano of the *panache*. He desires to be "admirable in all"—and only for his own satisfaction. This is the explanation of his profound sincerity. Even though he may reiterate many times that it is beauty which he loves, Cyrano loves sincerity and courage above all. He loves Christian mainly because he has made his promise to Roxane to protect him, but also because Christian is courageous. He loves Le Bret because he is sincere. He loves the cadets because they personify courage. He loves the pastry cook, Ragueneau, because he is a poet and writes sonnnets on the paper bags in which he wraps his tarts and pies. Cyrano's attitude toward women is the same: he shows esteem for a woman of the lowest social rank and treats her as a princess because she is kind and generous, but he has no sympathy for

---

30. **motley** composed of different or clashing elements
31. **bravuras** bold displays of daring
32. **gratuitous** without obligation; unnecessary; unearned
33. **poignantly** sensitively

Ragueneau's wife because she is harsh and insensitive to his poetry and treats her husband badly.

With regard to Roxane, Cyrano has a completely different outlook. At the beginning, his passion is a kind of poetic veneration[34] for her beauty; in her presence he remains wide-eyed and timid. When he learns that it is not himself but rather Christian who is loved by Roxane, his passion increases to the point of becoming poetry for the sake of love. Passion renders Cyrano heroic because it infuses into his noble heart the fire and warmth of his altruistic philosophy:

> . . . Self drops out of sight.
> For thy least good I would give all my own;—
> Aye, though thou knewst it not. . . .

Cyrano loves love more than he loves Roxane, but for him love is Roxane herself. His love is that of a man who has never known a woman intimately. He admits that he has never known "feminine sweetness."

At times, Cyrano is melancholy, but only toward the end of his life, as, for example, when Le Bret notices that he seems to be suffering. Cyrano starts, and cries out that he will never show others his suffering. All must appear heroic. During Roxane's last visit, looking at the falling leaves, he exclaims: "How well they fall!" and later he speaks of "the fullness of Fate's mockery." Cyrano is a man, a hero, from the beginning of the play to the end. He is Gascon only in appearance; within, he is a southerner, litigious,[35] passionate, and a lover of theatrical poses. His is the temperament of Don Quixote.

As for Roxane, she is affected, very light, with little spiritual depth. She is romantic, but without the youthful simplicity of Sylvette in *Romantics*. Her beauty is legendary, like the far-off princess Melissinde's, and her lace handkerchief inspires the starving garrison at the siege of Arras just as the vision of the princess far away encouraged the feverish sailors to continue rowing. Roxane further resembles Melissinde in that neither would ever consider committing a great crime of love. Roxane seeks only an excessively refined sort of love. Little by little, however, the influence of Cyrano's idealism has an impact on her concept of life's values, giving rise to a deep spiritual evolution within her. Ultimately, she is able to say to Christian: "At last I love thee for thy soul alone!" After Christian's death, she is faced with the cruel reality that there is nothing left in life for her, but she maintains an admirable calm. Subsequently, when she learns of Cyrano's love and exclaims: "I loved but once, and twice I lose my love!" although the concept

---

34. **veneration** feeling of deep respect and reverence
35. **litigious** quarrelsome

is affected, the cry comes from a heart genuinely in despair, and Roxane is tragically moving. In sum, the figure of the heroine represents a force in Cyrano's life; she is love personified. Just as Bertrand, in *The Princess Far Away*, is not easily defined or explained with respect to Melissinde, so the figure of Roxane is not easily juxtaposed[36] with respect to Cyrano.

Turning to the secondary characters as conceived by Rostand, Christian de Neuvillette may be defined as a provincial[37] youth, a bit out of style, who does not dare to speak to Roxane because he knows he lacks wit. He is very handsome and certainly is courageous because he dares to do something that no other brave soldier would even consider: tease Cyrano about his nose! But he is a simple soldier. He becomes impatient in the role of the affected lover, yet when Cyrano leaves him to his own devices, he is unable to do more than stammer some banalities.[38] In the end, he allows himself to be killed in the siege in order to leave an open, free path for his friend. Christian is genuinely sincere—and therefore is beloved by Cyrano—but his role is reduced to being handsome and consequently being nothing but an obstacle in Cyrano's love life. In this respect, he is the counterpart of Bertrand in *The Princess Far Away*.

Le Bret plays the role of the confidant. Embodying a spirit of good sense, he is a kind of Sancho Panza[39] at the side of Don Quixote.[40] Through the intimate conversations between Le Bret and Cyrano, the latter's character is developed and his ideas and ideals are revealed.

The last of the secondary characters is the Count de Guiche, a true cavalier in Louis XII style, typifying the role of the mundane in comedy. He lacks ideals, except for a sort of personal concept of *noblesse oblige*,[41] but his courage in battle inspires admiration. The only effect that Cyrano's idealism produces in him is to render him a bit dreamy at the end of the play, when he pronounces Cyrano's eulogy. His dreaminess, however, is not an early manifestation of the purification of a soul, but rather the expression of a weak and egotistic character that feels some remorse:

> Envious . . . Yes!
> Sometimes, when one has made life's success,
> One feels,—not finding, God knows, much amiss,—

---

36. **juxtaposed**   put side by side
37. **provincial**   countrified; rural; rustic
38. **banalities**   trite or commonplace statements
39. **Sancho Panza**   practical servant in Cervantes' *Don Quixote*
40. **Don Quixote**   Cervantes' character who, blinded to reality, seeks to right all wrong
41. ***noblesse oblige***   obligation of people of high rank to behave nobly or kindly to others

A thousand small distastes, whose sum is this;
Not quite remorse, but an obscure disorder.

Groups and crowds of personages are part of the play, and indeed Rostand shows extraordinary skill in harmonizing large numbers of onlookers with the action of the main characters. The dramatic duel scene and the exit procession are the most striking in *Cyrano de Bergerac*; the pastry cook surrounded by poets and cadets creates an additional unforgettable scene; and, finally, the group scene in the convent garden, under falling leaves, forms a scene of peace and tranquil joy mixed with a nuance[42] of fatality.

Undoubtedly there are some defects in Rostand's masterpiece: too much refinement, too many theatrical gestures. Cyrano is perhaps too much the incarnation of the Romantic hero, with his contrasting physical ugliness and moral beauty. The poetry of the play is pure and lyric, however, because it is sincere. Rostand, the excessively refined stylist, is comfortable in his own preciosity.[43] Rostand, the singer of heroic zeal, is comfortable in his Cyrano. The work, therefore, vibrates with preciosity, heroism, and poetic idealism. Moreover, as Patricia Williams maintains, the play is a strictly classical work in that it is faithful to the Aristotelian precepts,[44] one of which is that a tragedy must be plausible. She affirms that Cyrano "is completely credible, and his actions are completely motivated by his convictions. He is true to life."

The best excuse for Rostand's rhetoric[45] and the best compliment to his dramatic sense are offered, however, by T. S. Eliot, who writes:

> His rhetoric, at least, suited him at all times so well, and so much better than it suited a much greater poet, Baudelaire, who is at times as rhetorical as Rostand. . . . Is not Cyrano exactly in th[e] position of contemplating himself as a romantic, a dramatic figure? This dramatic sense on the part of the characters themselves is rare in modern drama. . . . Rostand had—whether he had anything else or not—this dramatic sense, and it is what gives life to Cyrano. It is a sense which is almost a sense of humour (for when any one is conscious of himself as acting, something like a sense of humour is present). It gives Rostand's characters—Cyrano at least—a gusto which is uncommon on the modern stage. . . . [I]n the particular case of Cyrano

---

42. **nuance** hint
43. **preciosity** great fastidiousness; overrefinement
44. **precepts** rules; directions
45. **rhetoric** art of using words effectively

on Noses, the character, the situation, the occasion were perfectly suited and combined. The tirade[46] generated by this combination is not only genuinely and highly dramatic: it is possibly poetry also.

Rostand's *Cyrano of Bergarac* will continue to have meaning throughout the ages, will continue to move audiences everywhere, and probably will remain identified with the name of Edmond Rostand long after his other works have sunk into complete oblivion.

---

46. **tirade** long vehement speech

Max Beerbohm

from
Around
Theatres

*From 1898 until 1910, Max Beerbohm was the drama
critic for London's* Saturday Review. *His wit and satire
are evident in these two reviews of* Cyrano de Bergerac.
*The first includes Beerbohm's opinion of the original pro-
duction, the second his less favorable opinion of the trans-
lation of the play into English.*

"Cyrano de Bergerac"

July 9, 1898

THE TRICOLOUR FLOATS over the Lyceum, and the critics are debating, with such animation as they can muster . . . for a play written in a
language to which they secretly prefer their own, whether "Cyrano" be a
classic. Paris has declared it to be a classic, and, international courtesy
apart, July is not the month for iconoclasm.[1] And so the general tendency
is to accept "Cyrano" in the spirit in which it has been offered to us. I
myself go with that tendency. Even if I could, I would not whisk from the
brow of M. Rostand, the talented boy-playwright, the laurels which Paris
has so reverently imposed on it. For, even if "Cyrano" be not a classic, it
is at least a wonderfully ingenious counterfeit of one, likely to deceive
experts far more knowing than I am. M. Rostand is not a great original
genius like (for example) M. Maeterlinck.[2] He comes to us with no marvelous revelation, but he is a gifted, adroit[3] artist, who does with freshness
and great force things that have been done before; and he is, at least, a

---

1. **iconoclasm** attacking widely accepted ideas
2. **Maurice Maeterlinck** Belgian poet and dramatist
3. **adroit** skillful; clever

monstrous fine fellow. His literary instinct is almost as remarkable as his instinct for the *technique*—the *pyrotechnique*[4]—of the theatre, insomuch that I can read "Cyrano" almost as often, with almost as much pleasure, as I could see it played. Personally, I like the Byzantine[5] manner in literature better than any other, and M. Rostand is nothing if not Byzantine: his lines are loaded and encrusted with elaborate phrases and curious conceits,[6] which are most fascinating to any one who, like me, cares for such things. Yet, strange as it seems, none of these lines is amiss in the theatre. All the speeches blow in gusts of rhetoric straight over the footlights into the very lungs of the audience. Indeed, there is this unusual feature in M. Rostand's talent, that he combines with all the verbal preciosity[7] of extreme youth the romantic ardour and technical accomplishment of middle-age. . . . If you have any sensibility to romance, you admire him so immensely as to be sure that whatever he may have done was for the best. All the characters and all the incidents in the play have been devised for the glorification of Cyrano, and are but, as who should say, so many rays of lime-light converging upon him alone. And that is as it should be. The romantic play which survives the pressure of time is always that which contains some one central figure, to which everything is subordinate—a one-part play, in other words. The part of Cyrano is one which, unless I am much mistaken, the great French actor in every future generation will desire to play. Cyrano will soon crop up in opera and in ballet. Cyrano is, in fact, as inevitably a fixture in romance as Don Quixote[8] or Don Juan,[9] Punch[10] or Pierrot.[11] Like them, he will never be out of date. But prophecy is dangerous? Of course it is. That is the whole secret of its fascination. Besides, I have a certain amount of reason in prophesying on this point. Realistic figures perish necessarily with the generation in which they were created, and their place is taken by figures typical of the generation which supervenes. But romantic figures belong to no period, and time does not dissolve them. Already Ibsen[12] is rather out of date—even Mr. Archer has washed his hands of Ibsen—while the elder Dumas[13] is still thoroughly in

---

4. **pyrotechnique** dazzling display of eloquence and wit
5. **Byzantine** characterized by complexity, deviousness, intrigue
6. **conceits** fanciful or witty expressions
7. **preciosity** great fastidiousness; overrefinement
8. **Don Quixote** hero, a visionary idealist, created by the Spanish novelist Cervantes
9. **Don Juan** legendary Spanish hero, known for his romantic endeavors
10. **Punch** hero of English puppet shows
11. **Pierrot** favorite of Italian drama and pantomime
12. **Henrik Ibsen** Norwegian playwright, often called the father of modern drama
13. **Alexander Dumas** French author of The *Three Musketeers* and *The Count of Monte Cristo*

touch with the times. Cyrano will survive because he is practically a new type in drama. I know that the motives of self-sacrifice-in-love and of beauty-adored-by-a-grotesque are as old, and as effective, as the hills, and have been used in literature again and again. I know that self-sacrifice is the motive of most successful plays. But, so far as I know, beauty-adored-by-a-grotesque has never been used with the grotesque as stage-hero. At any rate it has never been used so finely and so tenderly as by M. Rostand, whose hideous swashbuckler with the heart of gold and the talent for improvising witty or beautiful verses—Caliban[14] + Tartarin[15] + Sir Galahad[16] + Theodore Hook[17] was the amazing recipe for his concoction—is far too novel, I think, and too convincing, and too attractive, not to be permanent. Whether, in the meantime, Cyrano's soul has, as M. Rostand gracefully declares, passed into "vous, Coquelin,"[18] I am not quite sure. I should say that some of it—the comic, which is, perhaps, the greater part of it—has done so. But I am afraid that the tragic part is still floating somewhere, unembodied. Perhaps the two parts will never be embodied together in the same actor. Certainly, the comic part will never have a better billet[19] than its first.

I have said that the play is unlikely to suffer under the lapse of time. But though it has no special place in time, in space it has its own special place. It is a work charged with its author's nationality, and only the compatriots of its author can to the full appreciate it. Much of its subtlety and beauty must necessarily be lost upon us others. To translate it into English were a terrible imposition to set any one, and not even the worst offender in literature deserves such a punishment. To adapt it were harder than all the seven labours of Hercules rolled into one, and would tax the guile and strength of even Mr. Louis Parker. The characters in the "Chemineau" had no particular racial characteristics, and their transportation to Dorsetshire did them no harm. But there is no part of England which corresponds at all to the Midi.[20] An adapter of "Cyrano" might lay the scene in Cornwall, call the play "Then shall Cyrano die?" and write in a sixth act with a chorus of fifty thousand Cornishmen bent on knowing the reason why, or he might lay it in any of the other characteristic counties of England, but I should not like to answer for the consequences. However, the play will of

---

14. **Caliban** deformed, half-human slave in Shakespeare's *The Tempest*
15. **Tartarin** comic character in novels by French author Alphonse Daudet
16. **Sir Galahad** the purest and noblest knight of King Arthur's Round Table
17. **Theodore Hook** English playwright and novelist
18. ***vous, Coquelin*** "you, Coquelin"; Coquelin was the French actor who played Cyrano
19. **billet** situation; assigned place
20. **Midi** southern France

course be translated as it stands. And, meanwhile, no one should neglect this opportunity of seeing the original production. There is so much action in the piece, and the plot itself is so simple, that even those who know no French at all can enjoy it. And the whole setting of the piece is most delightful. I was surprised on the first night to see how excellent was the stage management. Except a pair of restive and absurd horses, there was no hitch, despite the difference of the Lyceum and the Porte Saint Martin. Why, by the way, are real horses allowed on the stage, where their hoofs fall with a series of dull thuds which entirely destroy illusion? Cardboard horses would be far less of a nuisance and far more convincing. However, that is a detail. I wish all my readers to see "Cyrano." It may not be the masterpiece I think it, but at any rate it is one's money's-worth. The stalls are fifteen shillings a-piece, but there are five acts, and all the five are fairly long, and each of them is well worth three shillings. Even if one does not like the play, it will be something, hereafter, to be able to bore one's grandchildren by telling them about Coquelin as Cyrano.

"Cyrano" in English

April 28, 1900

ONE EVENING, some years ago, I had been dining with a friend who was supposed to have certain spiritualistic powers. As we were very much bored with each other, I proposed that we should have a *séance*. Though doubtful whether I should be "sympathetic," he was quite willing to try. The question arose, with what spirit should we commune? He suggested Madame Blavatsky.[21] I was all for Napoleon Buonaparte. Finally—by what process I forget—we agreed on Charlotte Corday.[22] The lights having been turned out, we sat down at a small table. Placing the tips of our fingers on it, we thought of Charlotte Corday with all our might. Many minutes went slowly by, and the table showed no signs of animation. My friend said it was very strange. After a fruitless hour or so, he seemed to be so much annoyed that I thought it would be only kind to press my fingers in such a way as to make the table tilt duly towards me for a moment and then tilt back. I did this. "Are you there?" asked my friend, in a low voice. I pressed again, producing the requisite number of taps for "Yes." "Who are you?" my friend rejoined. "Charlotte" I rapped out. I continued to rap appropriate

---

21. **Madame Blavatsky** Russian-born spiritualist medium, magician, and occultist
22. **Charlotte Corday** assassin of Jean-Paul Marat, a radical politician during the French Revolution

answers to my friend until I thought he had had enough enjoyment for one evening. The spirit having evidently withdrawn to its own sphere, he turned up the lights, pronounced the *séance* a great success, and told me that I seemed to have some power as a medium. But I have never taken the advice he gave me to develop this power, and I recall our evening merely because I was irresistibly reminded of it, the other night, when I saw the English version of "Cyrano" at Wyndham's Theatre. I saw, with my mind's eye, the manner in which the whole play was written. There were Mr. Stuart Ogilvie and Mr. Louis N. Parker, seated solemnly on either side of a small table, trying to raise the spirit of Cyrano. "It is very strange," said Mr. Ogilvie, frowning; "the table does not seem to move." Genial Mr. Parker, hating that his friend should be disappointed, brought illicit pressure to bear on the table. "Are you there?" asked the author of "Hypatia," in a broken whisper. "Yes," rapped Mr. Parker, smiling inwardly. And so the mockery was inaugurated. So the collaboration went forward, hollow rap by rap, laboriously, portentously,[23] with no more real evocation than was got in the *séance* I have described.

Alas, that any pretence of raising this ghost need have been made among us! When first M. Coquelin brought M. Rostand's play to England I expressed a pious hope that it would not be translated. Of course, I knew well that it would be. Cyrano, the man, got safely home from the Hôtel de Bourgogne, routing with his own sword the hundred rascals who lay in wait for him; but Cyrano, the play, would not escape its English obsessors so easily. It might slip through the fingers of one and another of the hundred desperate actors who were thirsting to produce it. It might keep the whole gang at bay for a while. But in the end it would, inevitably, be taken. And, of course, it could only be taken dead: the nature of things prevented it from being taken alive. I dare say that I explained that fact at the time. But of what use was it to argue against a foregone conclusion? Cyrano, in the original version, is the showiest part of modern times—of any times, maybe. Innumerable limelights, all marvellously brilliant, converge on him. And as he moves he flashes their obsequious[24] radiance into the uttermost corners of the theatre. The very footlights, as he passes them, burn with a pale, embarrassed flame, useless to him as stars to the sun. The English critic, not less than the English actor, is dazzled by him. But, though he shut his eyes, his brain still works, and he knows well that an English version of Cyrano would be absurd. Cyrano, as a man, belongs to a particular province of France, and none but a Frenchman can really appreciate him. An Englishman can accept the Gascon, take him for granted, in a French

---

23. **portentously** ponderously; heavily
24. **obsequious** compliant; dutiful

version, but not otherwise. Cyrano is a local type; not, like Quixote or Juan, a type of abstract humanity which can pass unscathed through the world. Nor is he, like Quixote or Juan, a possible individual, such as one might meet. Even in Gascony he were impossible. He is the fantastically idealised creation of a poet. In M. Rostand's poetry, under the conditions which that poetry evokes, he is a real and solid figure, certainly. But put him into French prose, and what would remain of him but a sorry, disjointed puppet? Put him into English prose (or into the nearest English equivalent that could be found for M. Rostand's verse) and—but the result, though it can be seen at Wyndham's Theatre, cannot be described. All this I foresaw, being a critic. But the actors, not they. Creatures of impulse, they saw nothing but the chance of playing Cyrano. Mr. Wyndham happens to be the man who ultimately got it. But as the part does not, from a critic's standpoint, exist, how am I to praise his performance of it? how, as one who revels in his acting, do aught[25] but look devoutly forward to his next production?

---

25. **aught** anything whatever

Alice Walker

Beauty: When the Other Dancer Is the Self

In this memoir award-winning author Alice Walker tells of the impact a physical disability has had on her life.

It IS A BRIGHT SUMMER DAY in 1947. My father, a fat, funny man with beautiful eyes and a subversive wit, is trying to decide which of his eight children he will take with him to the county fair. My mother, of course, will not go. She is knocked out from getting most of us ready: I hold my neck stiff against the pressure of her knuckles as she hastily completes the braiding and then beribboning of my hair.

My father is the driver for the rich old white lady up the road. Her name is Miss Mey. She owns all the land for miles around, as well as the house in which we live. All I remember about her is that she once offered to pay my mother thirty-five cents for cleaning her house, raking up piles of her magnolia leaves, and washing her family's clothes, and that my mother—she of no money, eight children, and a chronic earache—refused it. But I do not think of this in 1947. I am two and a half years old. I want to go everywhere my daddy goes. I am excited at the prospect of riding in a car. Someone has told me fairs are fun. That there is room in the car for only three of us doesn't faze me at all. Whirling happily in my starchy frock, showing off my biscuit-polished patent-leather shoes and lavender socks, tossing my head in a way that makes my ribbons bounce, I stand, hands on hips, before my father. "Take me, Daddy," I say with assurance; "I'm the prettiest!"

Later, it does not surprise me to find myself in Miss Mey's shiny black car, sharing the back seat with the other lucky ones. Does not surprise me that I thoroughly enjoy the fair. At home that night I tell the unlucky ones all I can remember about the merry-go-round, the man who eats live chickens, and the teddy bears, until they say: that's enough baby Alice. Shut up now, and go to sleep.

It is Easter Sunday, 1950. I am dressed in a green, flocked, scalloped-hem dress (handmade by my adoring sister, Ruth) that has its own smooth satin petticoat and tiny hot-pink roses tucked into each scallop. My shoes, new T-strap patent leather, again highly biscuit-polished. I am six years old and have learned one of the longest Easter speeches to be heard that day, totally unlike the speech I said when I was two: "Easter lilies / pure and white / blossom in / the morning light." When I rise to give my speech I do so on a great wave of love and pride and expectation. People in the church stop rustling their new crinolines.[1] They seem to hold their breath. I can tell they admire my dress, but it is my spirit, bordering on sassiness (womanishness), they secretly applaud.

"That girl's a little *mess*," they whisper to each other, pleased.

Naturally I say my speech without stammer or pause, unlike those who stutter, stammer, or, worst of all, forget. This is before the word "beautiful" exists in people's vocabulary, but "Oh, isn't she the *cutest* thing?" frequently floats my way. "And got so much sense!" they gratefully add . . . for which thoughtful addition I thank them to this day.

It was great fun being cute. But then, one day, it ended.

I am eight years old and a tomboy. I have a cowboy hat, cowboy boots, checkered shirt and pants, all red. My playmates are my brothers, two and four years older than I. Their colors are black and green, the only difference in the way we are dressed. On Saturday nights we all go to the picture show, even my mother; Westerns are her favorite kind of movie. Back home, "on the ranch," we pretend we are Tom Mix, Hopalong Cassidy, Lash LaRue (we've even named one of our dogs Lash LaRue); we chase each other for hours rustling cattle, being outlaws, delivering damsels from distress. Then my parents decide to buy my brothers guns. These are not "real" guns. They shoot "BBs," copper pellets my brothers say will kill birds. Because I am a girl, I do not get a gun. Instantly I am relegated to the position of Indian. Now there appears a great distance between us. They shoot and shoot at everything with their new guns. I try to keep up with my bow and arrows.

One day while I am standing on top of our makeshift "garage"—pieces

---

1. **crinolines** petticoats made of coarse, stiff cloth, worn under skirts to make them puff out

of tin nailed across some poles—holding my bow and arrow and looking out toward the fields, I feel an incredible blow in my right eye. I look down just in time to see my brother lower his gun.

Both brothers rush to my side. My eye stings, and I cover it with my hand. "If you tell," they say, "we will get a whipping. You don't want that to happen, do you?" I do not. "Here is a piece of wire," says the older brother, picking it up from the roof; "say you stepped on one end of it and the other flew up and hit you." The pain is beginning to start. "Yes," I say. "Yes, I will say that is what happened." If I do not say this is what happened, I know my brothers will find ways to make me wish I had. But now I will say anything that gets me to my mother.

Confronted by our parents we stick to the lie agreed upon. They place me on a bench on the porch and I close my left eye while they examine the right. There is a tree growing from underneath the porch that climbs past the railing to the roof. It is the last thing my right eye sees. I watch as its trunk, its branches, and then its leaves are blotted out by the rising blood.

I am in shock. First there is intense fever, which my father tries to break using lily leaves bound around my head. Then there are chills: my mother tries to get me to eat soup. Eventually, I do not know how, my parents learn what has happened. A week after the "accident" they take me to see a doctor. "Why did you wait so long to come?" he asks, looking into my eye and shaking my head. "Eyes are sympathetic," he says. "If one is blind, the other will likely become blind too."

This comment of the doctor's terrifies me. But it is really how I look that bothers me most. Where the BB pellet struck there is a glob of whitish scar tissue, a hideous cataract, on my eye. Now when I stare at people—a favorite pastime, up to now—they will stare back. Not at the "cute" little girl, but at her scar. For six years I do not stare at anyone, because I do not raise my head.

Years later, in the throes of a mid-life crisis, I ask my mother and sister whether I changed after the "accident." "No," they say, puzzled. "What do you mean?"

What do I mean?

I am eight, and, for the first time, doing poorly in school, where I have been something of a whiz since I was four. We have just moved to the place where the "accident" occurred. We do not know any of the people around us because this is a different county. The only time I see the friends I knew is when we go back to our old church. The new school is the former state penitentiary. It is a large stone building, cold and drafty, crammed to overflowing with boisterous, ill-disciplined children. On the third floor there is a huge circular imprint of some partition that has been torn out.

"What used to be here?" I ask a sullen girl next to me on our way past it to lunch.

"The electric chair," says she.

At night I have nightmares about the electric chair; and about all the people reputedly "fried" in it. I am afraid of the school, where the students seem to be budding criminals.

"What's the matter with your eye?" they ask, critically.

When I don't answer (I cannot decide whether it was an "accident" or not), they shove me, insist on a fight.

My brother, the one who created the story about the wire, comes to my rescue. But then brags so much about "protecting" me, I become sick.

After months of torture at the school, my parents decide to send me back to our old community, to my old school. I live with my grandparents and the teacher they board.[2] But there is no room for Phoebe, my cat. By the time my grandparents decide there *is* room, and I ask for my cat, she cannot be found. Miss Yarborough, the boarding teacher, takes me under her wing, and begins to teach me to play the piano. But soon she marries an African—a "prince," she says—and is whisked away to his continent.

At my old school there is at least one teacher who loves me. She is the teacher who "knew me before I was born" and bought my first baby clothes. It is she who makes life bearable. It is her presence that finally helps me turn on the one child at the school who continually calls me [names]. One day I simply grab him by his coat and beat him until I am satisfied. It is my teacher who tells me my mother is ill.

My mother is lying in bed in the middle of the day, something I have never seen. She is in too much pain to speak. She has an abscess in her ear. I stand looking down on her, knowing that if she dies, I cannot live. She is being treated with warm oils and hot bricks held against her cheek. Finally a doctor comes. But I must go back to my grandparents' house. The weeks pass but I am hardly aware of it. All I know is that my mother might die, my father is not so jolly, my brothers still have their guns, and I am the one sent away from home.

"You did not change," they say.

Did I imagine the anguish of never looking up?

I am twelve. When relatives come to visit I hide in my room. My cousin Brenda, just my age, whose father works in the post office and whose mother is a nurse, comes to find me. "Hello," she says. And then she asks, looking at my recent school picture, which I did not want taken, and on which the

---

2. **board** provide with room and meals, for pay

"glob," as I think of it, is clearly visible, "You still can't see out of that eye?"

"No," I say, and flop back on the bed over my book.

That night, as I do almost every night, I abuse my eye. I rant and rave at it, in front of the mirror. I plead with it to clear up before morning. I tell it I hate and despise it. I do not pray for sight. I pray for beauty.

"You did not change," they say.

I am fourteen and baby-sitting for my brother Bill, who lives in Boston. He is my favorite brother and there is a strong bond between us. Understanding my feelings of shame and ugliness he and his wife take me to a local hospital, where the "glob" is removed by a doctor named O. Henry. There is still a small bluish crater where the scar tissue was, but the ugly white stuff is gone. Almost immediately I become a different person from the girl who does not raise her head. Or so I think. Now that I've raised my head I win the boyfriend of my dreams. Now that I've raised my head I have plenty of friends. Now that I've raised my head classwork comes from my lips as faultlessly as Easter speeches did, and I leave high school as valedictorian,[3] most popular student, and *queen*, hardly believing my luck. Ironically, the girl who was voted most beautiful in our class (and was) was later shot twice through the chest by a male companion, using a "real" gun, while she was pregnant. But that's another story in itself. Or is it?

"You did not change," they say.

It is now thirty years since the "accident." A beautiful journalist comes to visit and to interview me. She is going to write a cover story for her magazine that focuses on my latest book. "Decide how you want to look on the cover," she says. "Glamorous, or whatever."

Never mind "glamorous," it is the "whatever" that I hear. Suddenly all I can think of is whether I will get enough sleep the night before the photography session: if I don't, my eye will be tired and wander, as blind eyes will.

At night in bed . . . I think up reasons why I should not appear on the cover of a magazine. "My meanest critics will say I've sold out," I say. "My family will now realize I write scandalous books."

"But what's the real reason you don't want to do this?" he asks.

"Because in all probability," I say in a rush, "my eye won't be straight."

"It will be straight enough," he says. Then, "Besides, I thought you'd made your peace with that."

And I suddenly remember that I have.

I remember:

I am talking to my brother Jimmy, asking if he remembers anything

_____

3. **valedictorian** student with the highest scholastic rank in a graduating class

unusual about the day I was shot. He does not know I consider that day the last time my father, with his sweet home remedy of cool lily leaves, chose me, and that I suffered and raged inside because of this. "Well," he says, "all I remember is standing by the side of the highway with Daddy, trying to flag down a car. A white man stopped, but when Daddy said he needed somebody to take his little girl to the doctor, he drove off."

I remember:

I am in the desert for the first time. I fall totally in love with it. I am so overwhelmed by its beauty, I confront for the first time, consciously, the meaning of the doctor's words years ago: "Eyes are sympathetic. If one is blind, the other will likely become blind too." I realize I have dashed about the world madly, looking at this, looking at that, storing up images against the fading of the light. *But I might have missed seeing the desert!* The shock of that possibility—and gratitude for over twenty-five years of sight—sends me literally to my knees. Poem after poem comes—which is perhaps how poets pray.

ON SIGHT

I am so thankful I have seen
The Desert
And the creatures in the desert
And the desert Itself.

The desert has its own moon
Which I have seen
With my own eye
There is no flag on it.

Trees of the desert have arms
All of which are always up
That is because the moon is up
The sun is up
Also the sky
The stars
Clouds
None with flags.

If there *were* flags, I doubt
The trees would point.
Would you?

But mostly, I remember this:

I am twenty-seven, and my baby daughter is almost three. Since her birth I have worried about her discovery that her mother's eyes are different from other people's. Will she be embarrassed? I think. What will she say? Every day she watches a television program called "Big Blue Marble." It begins with a picture of the earth as it appears from the moon. It is bluish, a little battered-looking, but full of light, with whitish clouds swirling around it. Every time I see it I weep with love, as if it is a picture of Grandma's house. One day when I am putting Rebecca down for her nap, she suddenly focuses on my eye. Something inside me cringes, gets ready to try to protect myself. All children are cruel about physical differences, I know from experience, and that they don't always mean to be is another matter. I assume Rebecca will be the same.

But no-o-o-o. She studies my face intently as we stand, her inside and me outside her crib. She even holds my face maternally between her dimpled little hands. Then, looking every bit as serious and lawyerlike as her father, she says, as if it may just possibly have slipped my attention: "Mommy, there's a *world* in your eye." (As in, "Don't be alarmed, or do anything crazy.") And then, gently, but with great interest: "Mommy, where did you *get* that world in your eye?"

For the most part, the pain left then. (So what, if my brothers grew up to buy even more powerful pellet guns for their sons and to carry real guns themselves. So what, if a young "Morehouse man" once nearly fell off the steps of Trevor Arnett Library because he thought my eyes were blue.) Crying and laughing I ran to the bathroom, while Rebecca mumbled and sang herself off to sleep. Yes indeed, I realized, looking into the mirror. There *was* a world in my eye. And I saw that it was possible to love it: that in fact, for all it had taught me of shame and anger and inner vision, I *did* love it. Even to see it drifting out of orbit in boredom, or rolling up out of fatigue, not to mention floating back at attention in excitement (bearing witness, a friend has called it), deeply suitable to my personality, and even characteristic of me.

That night I dream I am dancing to Stevie Wonder's song "Always" (the name of the song is really "As," but I hear it as "Always"). As I dance, whirling and joyous, happier than I've ever been in my life, another bright-faced dancer joins me. We dance and kiss each other and hold each other through the night. The other dancer has obviously come through all right, as I have done. She is beautiful, whole and free. And she is also me.

On Falling in Love

Robert Louis Stevenson

Renowned author Robert Louis Stevenson explores the mystery of falling in love.

"Lord, what fools these mortals be!"
—*A Midsummer-Night's Dream*

THERE IS ONLY ONE event in life which really astonishes a man and startles him out of his prepared opinions. Everything else befalls him very much as he expected. Event succeeds to event, with an agreeable variety indeed, but with little that is either startling or intense; they form together no more than a sort of background, or running accompaniment to the man's own reflections; and he falls naturally into a cool, curious, and smiling habit of mind, and builds himself up in a conception of life which expects tomorrow to be after the pattern of today and yesterday. He may be accustomed to the vagaries[1] of his friends and acquaintances under the influence of love. He may sometimes look forward to it for himself with an incomprehensible expectation. But it is a subject in which neither intuition nor the behaviour of others will help the philosopher to the truth. There is probably nothing rightly thought or rightly written on this matter of love that is not a piece of the person's experience. I remember an anecdote of a well-known French theorist, who was debating a point eagerly in his *cénacle*.[2] It was objected against him that he had never experienced love. Whereupon he arose, left the society, and made it a point not to return to it until he considered that he had supplied the defect. "Now," he remarked, on entering, "now I am in a position to continue the discussion." Perhaps he had not penetrated very deeply into the subject after all; but the story indicates right thinking, and may serve as apologue[3] to readers of this essay.

---

1. **vagaries** odd or eccentric conduct
2. *cénacle* close circle of friends or followers
3. **apologue** short story with a moral; fable

When at last the scales fall from his eyes, it is not without something of the nature of dismay that the man finds himself in such changed conditions. He has to deal with commanding emotions instead of the easy dislikes and preferences in which he has hitherto[4] passed his days; and he recognises capabilities for pain and pleasure of which he had not yet suspected the existence. Falling in love is the one illogical adventure, the one thing of which we are tempted to think as supernatural, in our trite and reasonable world. The effect is out of all proportion with the cause. Two persons, neither of them, it may be, very amiable or very beautiful, meet, speak a little, and look a little into each other's eyes. That has been done a dozen or so of times in the experience of either with no great result. But on this occasion all is different. They fall at once into that state in which another person becomes to us the very gist and centrepoint of God's creation, and demolishes our laborious theories with a smile; in which our ideas are so bound up with the one master-thought that even the trivial cares of our own person become so many acts of devotion, and the love of life itself is translated into a wish to remain in the same world with so precious and desirable a fellow-creature. And all the while their acquaintances look on in stupor, and ask each other, with almost passionate emphasis, what so-and-so can see in that woman, or such-an-one in that man? I am sure, gentlemen, I cannot tell you. For my part, I cannot think what the women mean. It might be very well, if the Apollo Belvedere should suddenly glow all over into life, and step forward from the pedestal with that godlike air of his. But of the misbegotten changelings[5] who call themselves men, and prate[6] intolerably over dinner-tables, I never saw one who seemed worthy to inspire love—no, nor read of any, except Leonardo da Vinci, and perhaps Goethe in his youth. About women I entertain a somewhat different opinion; but there, I have the misfortune to be a man.

There are many matters in which you may waylay Destiny, and bid him stand and deliver. Hard work, high thinking, adventurous excitement, and a great deal more that forms a part of this or the other person's spiritual bill of fare, are within the reach of almost anyone who can dare a little and be patient. But it is by no means in the way of everyone to fall in love. You know the difficulty Shakespeare was put into when Queen Elizabeth asked him to show Falstaff in love. I do not believe that Henry Fielding was ever in love. Scott, if it were not for a passage or two in *Rob Roy*, would give me very much the same effect. These are great names and (what is more to the purpose) strong, healthy, highstrung, and generous natures, of whom the reverse might

---

4. **hitherto** until this time
5. **changelings** children secretly put in the place of others, especially in folk tales
6. **prate** chatter

have been expected. As for the innumerable army of anemic and tailorish persons who occupy the face of this planet with so much propriety,[7] it is palpably absurd to imagine them in any such situation as a love-affair. A wet rag goes safely by the fire; and if a man is blind, he cannot expect to be much impressed by romantic scenery. Apart from all this, many lovable people miss each other in the world, or meet under some unfavourable star. There is the nice and critical moment of declaration to be got over. From timidity or lack of opportunity a good half of possible love cases never get so far, and at least another quarter do there cease and determine. A very adroit person, to be sure, manages to prepare the way and out with his declaration in the nick of time. And then there is a fine solid sort of man, who goes on from snub to snub; and if he has to declare forty times, will continue imperturbably declaring, amid the astonished consideration of men and angels, until he has a favourable answer. I daresay, if one were a woman, one would like to marry a man who was capable of doing this, but not quite one who had done so. It is just a little bit abject,[8] and somehow just a little bit gross; and marriages in which one of the parties has been thus battered into consent scarcely form agreeable subjects for meditation. Love should run out to meet love with open arms. Indeed, the ideal story is that of two people who go into love step for step, with a fluttered consciousness, like a pair of children venturing together into a dark room. From the first moment when they see each other, with a pang of curiosity, through stage after stage of growing pleasure and embarrassment, they can read the expression of their own trouble in each other's eyes. There is here no declaration properly so called; the feeling is so plainly shared, that as soon as the man knows what it is in his own heart, he is sure of what it is in the woman's.

This simple accident of falling in love is as beneficial as it is astonishing. It arrests the petrifying influence of years, disproves cold-blooded and cynical conclusions, and awakens dormant sensibilities. Hitherto the man had found it a good policy to disbelieve the existence of any enjoyment which was out of his reach; and thus he turned his back upon the strong, sunny parts of nature, and accustomed himself to look exclusively on what was common and dull. He accepted a prose ideal, let himself go blind of many sympathies by disuse; and if he were young and witty, or beautiful, wilfully forewent[9] these advantages. He joined himself to the following of what, in the old mythology of love, was prettily called *nonchaloir*; and in an odd mixture of feelings, a fling of self-respect, a preference for selfish liberty, and a great dash of that fear with which honest people regard serious interests,

---

7. **propriety** conformity; concern for what is proper
8. **abject** degraded; lacking in self-respect
9. **forewent** relinquished

kept himself back from the straightforward course of life among certain se-
lected activities. And now, all of a sudden, he is unhorsed, like St. Paul,
from his infidel affectation. His heart, which has been ticking accurate seconds for the last year, gives a bound and begins to beat high and irregularly
in his breast. It seems as if he had never heard or felt or seen until that moment; and by the report of his memory, he must have lived his past life between sleep or waking, or with the preoccupied attention of a brown study.
He is practically incommoded[10] by the generosity of his feelings, smiles
much when he is alone, and develops a habit of looking rather blankly upon
the moon and stars. But it is not at all within the province of a prose essayist
to give a picture of this hyperbolical[11] frame of mind; and the thing has been
done already, and that to admiration. In *Adelaide*, in Tennyson's *Maud*, and
in some of Heine's songs, you get the absolute expression of this midsummer
spirit. Romeo and Juliet were very much in love; although they tell me some
German critics are of a different opinion, probably the same who would
have us think Mercutio a dull fellow. Poor Antony was in love, and no mistake. That lay figure Marius, in *Les Misérables*, is also a genuine case in his
own way, and worth observation. A good many of George Sand's people are
thoroughly in love; and so are a good many of George Meredith's. Altogether, there is plenty to read on the subject. If the root of the matter be in him,
and if he has the requisite chords to set in vibration, a young man may occa-
sionally enter, with the key of art, into that land of Beulah which is upon
the borders of Heaven and within sight of the City of Love. There let him
sit awhile to hatch delightful hopes and perilous illusions.

One thing that accompanies the passion in its first blush is certainly difficult to explain. It comes (I do not quite see how) that from having a very
supreme sense of pleasure in all parts of life—in lying down to sleep, in waking, in motion, in breathing, in continuing to be—the lover begins to regard
his happiness as beneficial for the rest of the world and highly meritorious[12]
in himself. Our race has never been able contentedly to suppose that the
noise of its wars, conducted by a few young gentlemen in a corner of an in-
considerable star, does not re-echo among the courts of Heaven with quite a
formidable effect. In much the same taste, when people find a great to-do in
their own breasts, they imagine it must have some influence in their neigh-
bourhood. The presence of the two lovers is so enchanting to each other
that it seems as if it must be the best thing possible for everybody else. They
are half inclined to fancy it is because of them and their love that the sky is
blue and the sun shines. And certainly the weather is usually fine while

---

10. **incommoded** bothered; made uncomfortable
11. **hyperbolic** exaggerated
12. **meritorious** deserving praise or reward

people are courting. . . . In point of fact, although the happy man feels very kindly towards others of his own sex, there is apt to be something too much of the magnifico[13] in his demeanour. If people grow presuming and self-important over such matters as a dukedom or the Holy See,[14] they will scarcely support the dizziest elevation in life without some suspicion of a strut; and the dizziest elevation is to love and be loved in return. Consequently, accepted lovers are a trifle condescending in their address to other men. An overweening sense of the passion and importance of life hardly conduces to simplicity of manner. To women, they feel very nobly, very purely, and very generously, as if they were so many Joan-of Arc's; but this does not come out in their behaviour; and they treat them to Grandisonian airs marked with a suspicion of fatuity.[15] I am not quite certain that women do not like this sort of thing; but really, after having bemused myself over *Daniel Deronda*, I have given up trying to understand what they like.

If it did nothing else, this sublime and ridiculous superstition, that the pleasure of the pair is somehow blessed to others, and everybody is made happier in their happiness, would serve at least to keep love generous and great-hearted. Nor is it quite a baseless superstition after all. Other lovers are hugely interested. They strike the nicest balance between pity and approval, when they see people aping the greatness of their own sentiments. It is an understood thing in the play that while the young gentlefolk are courting on the terrace, a rough flirtation is being carried on, and a light, trivial sort of love is growing up, between the footman and the singing chambermaid. As people are generally cast for the leading parts in their own imaginations, the reader can apply the parallel to real life without much chance of going wrong. In short, they are quite sure this other love-affair is not so deep-seated as their own, but they like dearly to see it going forward. And love, considered as a spectacle, must have attractions for many who are not of the confraternity.[16] The sentimental old maid is a commonplace of the novelists; and he must be rather a poor sort of human being, to be sure, who can look on at this pretty madness without indulgence and sympathy. For nature commends itself to people with a most insinuating art; the busiest is now and again arrested by a great sunset; and you may be as pacific or as cold-blooded as you will, but you cannot help some emotion when you read of well-disputed battles, or meet a pair of lovers in the lane.

Certainly, whatever it may be with regard to the world at large, this idea of beneficent pleasure is true as between the sweethearts. To do good and

---

13. **magnifico** person of high rank or great importance
14. **Holy See** papal seat; center of authority
15. **fatuity** stupidity; smug foolishness
16. **confraternity** brotherhood

communicate is the lover's grand intention. It is the happiness of the other that makes his own most intense gratification. It is not possible to disentangle the different emotions, the pride, humility, pity, and passion, which are excited by a look of happy love or an unexpected caress. To make one's self beautiful, to dress the hair, to excel in talk, to do anything and all things that puff out the character and attributes and make them imposing in the eyes of others, is not only to magnify one's self, but to offer the most delicate homage[17] at the same time. And it is in this latter intention that they are done by lovers; for the essence of love is kindness and indeed it may be best defined as passionate kindness: kindness, so to speak, run mad and become importunate[18] and violent. Vanity in a merely personal sense exists no longer. The lover takes a perilous pleasure in privately displaying his weak points and having them, one after another, accepted and condoned. He wishes to be assured that he is not loved for this or that good quality, but for himself, or something as like himself as he can contrive to set forward. For, although it may have been a very difficult thing to paint the marriage of Cana, or write the fourth act of *Antony and Cleopatra*, there is a more difficult piece of art before every one in this world who cares to set about explaining his own character to others. Words and acts are easily wrenched from their true significance; and they are all the language we have to come and go upon. A pitiful job we make of it, as a rule. For better or worse, people mistake our meaning and take our emotions at a wrong valuation. And generally we rest pretty content with our failures; we are content to be misapprehended by cackling flirts; but when once a man is moonstruck with this affection of love, he makes it a point of honour to clear such dubieties[19] away. He cannot have the Best of her Sex misled upon a point of this importance; and his pride revolts at being loved in a mistake.

He discovers a great reluctance to return on former periods of his life. To all that has not been shared with her, rights and duties, bygone fortunes and dispositions, he can look back only by a difficult and repugnant effort of the will. That he should have wasted some years in ignorance of what alone was really important, that he may have entertained the thought of other women with any show of complacency, is a [burden] almost too heavy for his self-respect. But it is the thought of another past that rankles in his spirit like a poisoned wound. That he himself made a fashion of being alive in the bald, beggarly days before a certain meeting, is deplorable enough in all good conscience. But that She should have permitted herself the same liberty seems inconsistent with a Divine providence.

---

17. **homage** respect; honor
18. **importunate** demanding
19. **dubieties** doubtful things

A great many people run down jealousy, on the score that it is an artificial feeling, as well as practically inconvenient. This is scarcely fair; for the feeling on which it merely attends, like an ill-humoured courtier, is itself artificial in exactly the same sense and to the same degree. I suppose what is meant by that objection is that jealousy has not always been a character of man; formed no part of that very modest kit of sentiments with which he is supposed to have begun the world; but waited to make its appearance in better days and among richer natures. And this is equally true of love, and friendship, and love of country, and delight in what they call the beauties of nature, and most other things worth having. Love, in particular, will not endure any historical scrutiny: to all who have fallen across it, it is one of the most incontestable facts in the world; but if you begin to ask what it was in other periods and countries, in Greece for instance, the strangest doubts begin to spring up, and everything seems so vague and changing that a dream is logical in comparison. Jealousy, at any rate, is one of the consequences of love; you may like it or not, at pleasure; but there it is.

It is not exactly jealousy, however, that we feel when we reflect on the past of those we love. A bundle of letters found after years of happy union creates no sense of insecurity in the present; and yet it will pain a man sharply. The two people entertain no vulgar doubt of each other: but this preexistence of both occurs to the mind as something indelicate. To be altogether right, they should have had twin birth together, at the same moment with the feeling that unites them. Then indeed it would be simple and perfect and without reserve or afterthought. Then they would understand each other with a fullness impossible otherwise. There would be no barrier between them of associations that cannot be imparted. They would be led into none of those comparisons that send the blood back to the heart. And they would know that there had been no time lost, and they had been together as much as was possible. For besides terror for the separation that must follow some time or other in the future, men feel anger, and something like remorse, when they think of that other separation which endured until they met. Someone has written that love makes people believe in immortality, because there seems not to be room enough in life for so great a tenderness, and it is inconceivable that the most masterful of our emotions should have no more than the spare moments of a few years. Indeed, it seems strange; but if we call to mind analogies, we can hardly regard it as impossible.

"The blind bow-boy," who smiles upon us from the end of terraces in old Dutch gardens, laughingly hails his bird-bolts among a fleeting generation. But for as fast as ever he shoots, the game dissolves and disappears into eternity from under his falling arrows; this one is gone ere he is struck; the other has but time to make one gesture and give one passionate cry; and they are all the things of a moment. When the generation is gone, when the play is over, when the thirty years' panorama has been withdrawn in tatters from the stage of the world, we may ask what has become of these great, weighty, and undying loves, and the sweethearts who despised mortal conditions in a fine credulity; and they can only show us a few songs in a bygone taste, a few actions worth remembering, and a few children who have retained some happy stamp from the disposition of their parents.

Esther Gwinnell

Strangers in Love

In Cyrano de Bergerac, Roxane falls in love with a man who reveals his soul in beautiful letters. In this reading, Esther Gwinnell describes other relationships that unfolded through letter writing and discusses the phenomenon of courtship through correspondence.

Letters to Soldiers

. . . People have fallen in love in every conceivable[1] situation, and some people who never met in person have fallen in love through the exchange of letters. This is what happened between Annie and Corporal Tom, a soldier stationed in Vietnam in 1967.

> *February 3, 1967*
>
> *Dear Annie,*
>
> *Sorry to be so long about writing back to you. Since your last letter, we have been slogging around in the jungle, and I haven't had any way to write to you. The VC[2] have been busy this week, gearing up for the usual Tet (that means "spring") offensive, and that has kept us on our toes. It's been raining nearly continuously, warm rain, the kind of rain that rots out your boots. Everybody here has some kind of foot fungus to go along with the constant dampness.*
>
> *Since I got your picture, I like to think about you standing in your garden. I like to think about your garden, too. I've been in this country so long that I find myself thinking of home and gardens like yours the same way I think about movies or books I've read. They don't seem quite real to me, but you seem real to me. Looking at you in the picture makes you seem more real than anything else around here. I can almost smell the roses.*
>
> *Is that a fruit tree behind you? Please tell me it's a peach tree! I*

---

1. **conceivable** imaginable
2. **VC** Vietcong

know I have already complained to you about the food, but that is the soldier's complaint. Food is rarely even what I used to consider edible, and some nights in the bunker, when I have one ear cocked for unusual noises, I drift into dreams about (don't laugh, now) peaches. Rich, luscious peaches still warm from the sun, the smell of them, the feel of the peach fuzz on my teeth.

I've been carrying your picture in my chest pocket, you know, the place where guys carry their Bibles in hopes of stopping that stray shot. Only now I've got you there, and I look at you a lot, trying to remind myself that home is real and that I am really going to get there again. I like to think about going to the drive-in with you, and eating hamburgers and drinking Coca-Cola delivered by carhops,[3] and the ground would be dry and my feet would be dry. When I get home, can I take you to the drive-in?

Sorry about the condition of this letter. I haven't got much paper available right now, and this is the worse for the wear. I'll try to find something better next time.

You know I can't wait to hear from you again, my home girl. Send me another piece of home soon (I know you can't send me a peach!).

Always yours,
Corporal Tom

(This letter, stained and wrinkled, received March 5, 1967)

Some four months after he sent this letter, Corporal Tom was wounded in Vietnam and was medically evacuated to the States. Annie met him at the airport, and later they went to that drive-in movie together. They married in the fall of 1968 and have celebrated more than twenty-five years of marriage. Sometimes, on a warm summer night when the peaches are ripe, they sit under the trees and talk about the letters they wrote, the letters that drew them together and how they fell in love long before they ever met in person.

During the Korean War and the Vietnam War, thousands of strangers met and corresponded through letters like these—then fell in love. *Dear Abby* has printed many letters from people who met through Operation Dear Abby, a letter drive for soldiers. The stories of their romances are often poignant[4] and sometimes funny, but always two people fell in love who were strangers to each other—strangers they knew only through the written word.

---

3. **carhops** waiters or waitresses at a drive-in restaurant
4. **poignant** touching

For Operation Dear Abby, schoolchildren wrote letters and young women wrote letters. The USO amassed[5] barrels of these letters and generally divided them by state of origin, so that the soldiers could choose letters from their home state. Sometimes those letters formed the basis for a relationship that resulted in love and marriage. One man told me of picking up a letter from a barrel had been wrongly filed—and answering it anyway. He later met the woman who wrote it, and they were married.

For soldiers, living in a world of danger, jungles and booby traps, these letters provided a remembrance of home, a sense of connection to ordinary life. The intensity of their yearning[6] for ordinary life fueled the importance they attached to the letters, and in the jungles and the mountains, under combat conditions, they wrote their own letters back to the unknown women.

Like Corporal Tom, many thought almost constantly about the letters and the letter writer, daydreaming about what they would do when they went home. They daydreamed of sitting under peach trees or going to a drive-in, sitting next to the woman. The daydreams fostered a still-greater sense of attachment, and the letter writer became a symbol for home, for the place in their daydreams where home existed.

Falling in love through letters is far different from falling in love face to face. With the letters to the soldiers, usually no face was attached to the writer; a soldier had no real information about who she was or what she looked like (unless she sent a photograph). In normal peacetime many of the writers would never have met in person. Their sense of shared common interest and common experiences came from the letters themselves.

A powerful sense of romance can spring from writing letters to someone you don't know and whose life is very different from yours. The idea of writing to a soldier, whose life is in constant danger, lends a fairy-tale quality to the writing. The strength of this feeling can make each letter valuable, even treasured. The woman's fear for the safety of the soldier, his longing for home, and their common daydreams about some future time of safety and even joy all combined to make these letters important in a way that took them out of the realm of the ordinary.

Not Entirely Strangers

Even from these almost-anonymous letters, the letter writers can learn many things about each other. For his part, the most obvious fact about him is that he is a soldier, in a foreign land. His name and rank can be found in his return address; he is likely to be between the ages of eighteen and

---

5. **amassed** collected
6. **yearning** feeling strong desire

twenty-five, and his situation can be imagined from news reports and from the physical condition of the letter pages.

The young woman writing these letters also supplies information about herself, often information she has no idea she is conveying. For example, she may write on humorous stationery or perfume her envelopes. She may use elegant paper, or she may write on notebook paper. Her ethnic heritage may be inferred from her name, and clues to her education and intellect may be found in her handwriting and spelling.

Especially under adverse[7] conditions, the character of the writers becomes evident. As Marsha remembers, "I knew Jeff was in combat a lot, and that the conditions were terrible. I don't know how he wrote to me so much. He must have spent every spare minute writing those letters—some of them were ten pages long, written very small and on both sides of the page. But you know, every letter he wrote had jokes in it, jokes that were going around or funny things he thought of to say about the guys in his unit, about the food or about the people in the villages.

"I thought to myself, here's this guy in the jungle somewhere, thinking of me. Here he is, every day hard and dangerous, and he still makes jokes! I think I fell in love with him for making jokes when everything around him was so awful. A guy like that, you know that he isn't going to be thrown by anything life hands him."

Marsha believed that she learned more about Jeff from those letters than she would have if she had first met him in person. When they did meet, he was very shy and quiet, and it took several dates before his shyness wore off enough for her to see the Jeff she knew from the letters. She knows that if she hadn't already known from his letters that the humor and strength were in there somewhere, she would never have had a second date with him. Now, every anniversary, their children happily tell the story of how Mom and Dad met through letters during the war.

Not all of the soldiers' stories have a fairy-tale ending. Some of their marriages ended after a few years, while others couldn't make the connection in person that they had made on paper. For a few of the soldiers, their feelings of love, formed under combat conditions, didn't survive the transition to coming home and reconnecting with their life before the war. Yet while they were in Korea or Vietnam, these soldiers had felt themselves to be deeply in love with their pen pals and spent their days and nights dreaming of the time when they would be together.

---

7. **adverse** difficult; unfavorable

Why Strangers Fall in Love

Several factors contributed to the development of loving relationships between the writers of these letters. One, as already noted, was the sense of
importance that these letters had to the writers. They were not ordinary
business correspondence, or casual letters between friends. They were letters between The War and Home, letters from danger to safety, letters that
seemed to form a lifeline between two people. Those who maintained the
correspondence invested their emotions in it: even if no romance was involved, they made a commitment to continue it.

Another factor is that many of the soldiers and the women were single.
They were likely close in age, and both had already made some effort to
reach out. This increased the likelihood that they were at least theoreti-
cally available for a relationship. Some soldiers corresponded with several
writers, and some of the women wrote letters to several soldiers. The situation was ripe for romantic relationships to develop between the authors
of these letters.

Finally, there is a magic to the written word. Receiving letters has a
mystique that is just not available in face-to-face relationships. If you look
in your closet, chances are that you have a small (or large!) bundle of love
letters from some period in your life, tied with a ribbon and carefully preserved. The words may be pretty mundane,[8] and the lover may long since
have left your life, but you can recall the memory of love from those letters
in a way that other forms of communication cannot duplicate.

With all these factors combined, it is hardly surprising that letter writers
became very attached to each other. But we are still left with the question of
how these men and women *fell in love* with strangers, people whom they had
never met before, whom they did not see or touch or smell. These strangers
had never spoken to each other on the phone and would not have recognized each other if they met on the street.

Corporal Tom's letter shows us some of the reasons he made that romantic connection with Annie. He daydreamed about her, and she filled his
thoughts whenever he needed something pleasant to think about. He could
have fantasies about her, filling in the gaps in his information about who
she was in real life with the qualities of his own ideal woman. She would
love dancing maybe, or she would really enjoy swimming at that beach he
always went to when he was sixteen. He invested[9] his fantasy life in Annie,
and she became for him an ideal woman because whatever he didn't know
about her—what she was like, how she moved, what her voice sounded
like—he could invent from his own daydreams.

---

8. **mundane** ordinary
9. **invested** devoted; gave time and effort of

Tom also built fantasies of a future with Annie as a way of avoiding thinking about his current situation. In this way he reassured himself that he would actually have a future, that he would someday get out of "this stinking jungle" and go back home to drive-in movies and peaches and a girl in a long dress in a garden.

Certainly, as they exchanged letters, he modified[10] his ideas about her. Annie actually didn't swim, but she did like dancing; she had cut her hair, and it was different from the picture. She was really into baking and was more of a homebody than he had imagined. But until they met in person, there would always be gaps in his knowledge of her.

For her part, Annie made up a picture of Tom based on television news reports showing soldiers in Vietnam. She originally had thought of him simply in uniform, like the soldiers she saw at a military base near her home. But the television pictures of soldiers were different; they were dirty and tired and their uniforms looked different—they were wearing camouflage or seemed to be only partly wearing uniforms. They looked hot and hadn't shaved. She saw one soldier that she thought of as being like Tom, and whenever she thought of Tom, it was this television image that she saw in her mind.

Both Tom and Annie were willing to feel deeply about each other without meeting. As they wrote to each other, they shared thoughts they had never shared with anyone else before. Annie wrote about her feelings about the war, and her sense of being a part of a bigger world than she had previously experienced, because a part of her was now connected to this soldier in Vietnam. Tom wrote about his experiences, and his sense of how he was changing because of those experiences. The process of writing to this stranger was deepening his introspection,[11] increasing his self-understanding in a way that was not possible anywhere else in his danger-filled life.

Using the letter writing as a form of diary keeping, Annie told Tom about her daily activities: about running into friends at the market, the movies she saw, the books she read, an argument she had with her mother. All were gratefully received. Although she wrote the letters for Tom, they also served her as a place to pause in her day and think about her world. In this sense, the letters served a therapeutic[12] need for them both.

By itself, this kind of intimacy would have increased the sense of connection between them. But the warmth of their letters and their mutual feeling of being listened to increased their intimacy,[13] until they both felt

---

10. **modified** changed
11. **introspection** examination of one's own thoughts and feelings
12. **therapeutic** curative; healing
13. **intimacy** deep understanding; closeness

that they were sharing from the soul. Letting down the barriers for intimacy lets down the barriers for caring and attachment; sharing secrets creates a bond. That bond, plus the daydreams and the magic of letters, led Annie and Tom to fall in love.

Their facelessness to each other actually contributed to the intimacy of the writing. Because no relationship had existed before, there was little risk for either Tom or Annie in being honest and open. They would not be running into each other at parties or at the grocery store. They would not be dealing in person with the real human being to whom they were writing. They could be as intimate with each other as they wanted and needed to be.

Annie, who wrote as though she were writing in her diary, had a sense that Tom was somehow an extension of herself. He would not be truly real to her until she met him in person. Until that time, she created an image of him based both on the information in his letters and on her own imagination.

Some famous diary keepers have also created an image of the person they were writing to. When Anne Frank wrote in her diary, she created a fictional character to write to, so that she could imagine an emotional connection between herself and "Kitty," her reader. Although Tom was certainly more real to Annie than Kitty was to Anne Frank, he was still essentially without form until their actual physical meeting.

This is not to suggest that the love that Annie and Tom felt for each other was anything less than deep, intense and abiding.[14] Had Tom been killed in combat instead of wounded, Annie would have grieved for his loss even if they never met, as she would have for anyone else she loved. But that grief would also have been different from her grief for someone she knew and loved in person.

Tangible[15] Evidence of Love

When I was in medical school and my then-boyfriend was in law school in another state, I waited for his letters with an eagerness that is hard to describe. Letters can be read again and again and be savored[16] and cherished in a way that phone calls cannot. I could write to him in the middle of the night (and often did), and I could reread his letters for comfort or company whenever I wanted.

It wasn't that his letters were masterpieces of the written word, or filled with poetry. They were just discussions of the day's activities, written in his own handwriting and carrying with them the flavor of who he was. But they

---

14. **abiding** enduring; continuing
15. **tangible** touchable; real
16. **savored** delighted in

were tangible proof of his existence—I could touch them and see them and read them when I was lonely. Every trip to the mailbox made me slightly anxious: Would there be a letter today? Or would I have to wait until tomorrow? I would hope for a really long letter, because it would take longer to read, and it would mean he had spent a lot of time writing it and thinking about me. The joy of finding a letter, or the disappointment of going away empty-handed—each day held the possibility of either outcome.

Being far from home and under a fair amount of stress, I would deeply appreciate every letter. I engaged in a lively correspondence with many friends from college, and it was a rare day that I had no mail at all. As special as the letters from my boyfriend were, all the letters I got from my friends were important, too.

Pen-pal Romances

Another way that people have met through letters alone is through having a pen pal. A fairly common activity for schoolchildren, writing to a pen pal is also popular among young adults who enjoy writing letters. A bit of a fantasy is always involved in writing to a pen pal, especially the fantasy that you will make a lifelong friend, preferably in some romantic and faraway place. (And of course, wherever *you* are will seem romantic and faraway to your pen pal.)

The method by which pen pals connect is similar to that of soldiers and the women back home. Generally, both writers are interested in having a pen pal. Among young people, the likelihood is greater that the pen pals will be of the same gender, if only because people who get pen pals seem predisposed to finding someone as like themselves as possible. Women tend to write to women, and more women (or girls) seem to want pen pals than men. But if they are of the right age and gender, pen pals can also fall in love.

Branwyn was fifteen years old and living in Ireland when she got a letter at school from a boy in New York whose class was doing a project on Irish history. Patrick was sixteen and of Irish heritage. He'd sent his letter to the mayor of the town his family came from, asking that it be forwarded to someone in the school who would be willing to help him. Branwyn collected stamps, so she ended up with the task of answering the letter in exchange for obtaining the stamps from it.

Over the next few years, Branwyn and Patrick wrote to each other a few times a month. Patrick would send her stamps that he collected just for her, and he would tell her about his day-to-day struggles with science classes and his dashed hopes of making first string on the football team. Quite a lively exchange occurred when it became clear to both of them that football meant something quite different to an Irish girl and an American boy.

There never seemed to be much likelihood that they would meet; their families were not wealthy, and neither had ever traveled outside their own country. But the letters continued, and the two became good friends. They sent each other their school pictures. Branwyn continued on to the university to study biology, and Patrick went on to take a job with an airline. Suddenly the possibility of meeting moved from daydream to reality. After four years of corresponding, they suddenly became aware of each other not just as good but long-distance friends, but also as possible lovers.

Branwyn dug out her old pictures of Patrick and reminded herself of his growth from boy to man. As they wrote back and forth sharing their fears and hopes about a possible meeting, their letters intensified in their emotional content. Some time had to pass before Patrick had put enough time in with the airline to fly to Ireland, which meant they had lots of time to get cold feet, to get panicked and to reassure themselves that they had been friends for years. Even if no relationship came out of the meeting, they could still have a good visit, and Branwyn would have a chance to show Patrick around his ancestral home.

Patrick, on his end, was looking daily at Branwyn's photograph. He found himself entranced with thoughts of her. He reread all her letters and laughed at the childish things they had once written. But when he finally came to Ireland, he was disconcerted[17] to find that he had a hard time understanding what she was saying, while she was taken aback by how tall he was. These differences between fantasy and reality were initially very difficult for both of them to deal with. But after only a few days Patrick was just as entranced with the real Branwyn as he had been with his pen pal.

On his second visit to Ireland, Patrick proposed marriage, and Branwyn accepted. With their parents' help, Branwyn transferred to a university in New York, and Patrick and Branwyn later married.

The relationship between Patrick and Branwyn has some features that are different from the soldiers' relationships with women back home. Obviously, neither one was in danger, and they were engaged in writing to each other as teenagers. In a sense, they grew up together. They never expected to be able to meet, and so their fantasies about each other were not "rehearsals" for a meeting. That lack of a possibility for meeting also freed them from restrictions on what they might say to each other.

In adolescence, many young people are driven to try to be "normal" or like the other teens around them. They hide their inner selves from one another, carefully watching to see whether their own feelings match those of the teens around them, fearing exposure as being "different," even while striving in some sense to be unique. For Patrick and Branwyn, this tendency

---

17. **disconcerted** taken aback

to hide from each other's scorn was reduced (though not absent) because they never thought they would really meet.

Still, their interaction had a romantic quality because they lived in different countries and were boy and girl—this is the stuff that movies are made of. The length of their correspondence is quite remarkable, and few of the Internet couples who responded to my questionnaire even came close to writing for five years before meeting. In the course of this correspondence, Branwyn and Patrick had essentially gone to school together and grown up together.

Both had daydreamed about the person they were writing to. Each created a mental image, one that incorporated information from the letters but that was also heavily based on books and movies about the other's country. When Patrick watched movies about Ireland, he thought of Branwyn. When Branwyn read books about America, she thought of Patrick. Over the years their exchange of photographs allowed them to visualize each other, but their ideas about how the other would talk, behave and even dress in real life were all fantasy.

Like the soldiers and their female pen pals, Patrick and Branwyn developed a degree of intimacy that was greater than the intimacy of any of their relationships in their day-to-day life. Fortunately for them, they were able to transfer that intimacy from letters to a face-to-face relationship. This does not always happen. The differences between daydream and reality can create a tremendous barrier between two people, even people who have already shared a great deal about themselves in writing. For an international couple like Patrick and Branwyn, the difference in their two cultures might have enhanced those barriers to the point that they would be uncomfortable with each other in person, even though writing back and forth had been easy. . . .

From the Post Office to the Internet

. . . Many teenagers who would once have formed relationships with teenagers in other countries as pen pals now meet their peers online. With the Internet, it is easy to write a note to a friend in England or Australia and to correspond with other young people throughout the world. Writing to someone living in another country has the same attraction over the Internet as in pen-pal correspondence, and e-mail provides the same sense of safety from peer judgment, enhanced by the ease of connecting.

But the differences between Internet relationships and ordinary letter-writing relationships are also important. Much of the nonverbal[18] information that can be gleaned from letters is not available in Internet communication. There is no handwriting, no stationery, no dependable return address and

---

18. **nonverbal** without spoken words

sometimes no real name to convey clues about the real person. Internet relationships begin with even more anonymity, and they progress without the social and personal clues that an ordinary letter would provide.

These similarities and differences between Internet relationships and other anonymous relationships are worth noting because the newness of Internet relationships may make them seem abnormal or strange. Yet in letters to soldiers [and] pen pals . . . we find the basic components of Internet relationships.